A General Sketch of the
New Testament
in the Light of
Christ and
the Church

WITNESS LEE

PART 2
ROMANS THROUGH PHILEMON

Living Stream Ministry
Anaheim, California • www.lsm.org

© 1999 Living Stream Ministry

First Edition, October 1999.

ISBN 0-7363-0186-0

Published by

Living Stream Ministry
2431 W. La Palma Ave., Anaheim, CA 92801 U.S.A.
P. O. Box 2121, Anaheim, CA 92814 U.S.A.

Printed in the United States of America

99 00 01 02 03 04 / 9 8 7 6 5 4 3 2 1

CONTENTS

Title	*Page*
Preface	v
9 Condemnation and Justification in Romans	95
10 Sanctification in Romans	103
11 Sanctification, Glorification, Selection, and the Body Life in Romans	115
12 The Main Principles in 1 Corinthians	131
13 The Principles and Cases in 1 Corinthians	143
14 The Ministry and the Ministers in 2 Corinthians	159
15 Walking by the Spirit in Galatians	173
16 Aspects of the Church in Ephesians	185
17 Crucial Points Concerning the Church in Ephesians	199
18 The Experience of Christ in Philippians	209
19 Christ as Everything in Colossians (1)	221
20 Christ as Everything in Colossians (2)	231
21 Faith, Love, and Hope in 1 and 2 Thessalonians	241
22 The Practice of the Church Life in 1 and 2 Timothy	253
23 The Practice of the Church Life in Titus and Philemon	265

PREFACE

This four-part series is composed of messages given by Brother Witness Lee in the summer of 1964. Parts one and two were given in New York City. Parts three and four were given in Los Angeles, California. These messages were not reviewed by the speaker.

CHAPTER NINE

CONDEMNATION AND JUSTIFICATION IN ROMANS

Scripture Reading: Rom. 1:28; 2:15, 17; 3:21-25; 4:25; 5:10-11

THE CONTENT AND SECTIONS OF ROMANS

The book of Romans is composed of five main sections. The fourth section, chapters nine through eleven may be considered as a parenthetical section, dealing with God's selection by grace. The four other main sections are condemnation, justification, sanctification (including conformation and glorification), and transformation for practicing the Body life. These are all structured in a very good sequence.

The first section, the section of condemnation, reveals that all mankind is in a fallen condition, condemned by God under His righteous law. The second section, on justification, clearly reveals that we are justified through the redemption of Christ. Concerning the third section, most Bible expositors use one word—*sanctification*. However, the word *sanctification* is not adequate to express the full content of this section. It is preferable to say that sanctification includes the processes of conformation to the image of the Son of God and glorification, the redemption of our body, in which we will be glorified together with Him (8:29, 17, 30). Having been justified, we are now in the process of sanctification and conformation until the day that the Lord comes back, when we will be glorified. These three matters are dealt with in this section.

Most students of the Scriptures pay attention only to sanctification; they neglect conformation and glorification. Regeneration is accomplished in our spirit, but 12:2 shows us that after the Lord regenerates us in our spirit, He transforms us in our soul. This means that our soul, our very being, must be conformed to the image of the Son of God. In addition, glorification is accomplished in our body. Hence, we experience sanctification and conformation in our soul and eventually glorification in our body.

The fifth main section of Romans continues the third section, dealing with our Christian walk. While we are in the process of transformation and conformation, and before the time of our glorification, we are living on the earth. The manner of our living is dealt with from chapter twelve through chapter sixteen. Although many things are covered in this section, the main thought is the Body life, the church life. Chapter twelve speaks of the Body life, and chapter sixteen reveals the genuine practice of the Body life, indicating that the first item of the Christian walk is the Body life, and the last item of the Christian walk is also the Body life. All the regenerated ones are members of Christ's Body. God's intention in transforming us is to make us the living, functioning members of His Body. The conclusion of Romans is that while we are here on this earth, we practice the Body life as His living, functioning members. This is the content and the sections of this book.

CONDEMNATION

Let us now look at some of the details in this book. In the first five books of the New Testament there is the history of the universal man, who is Christ as the Head and the church as the Body composed of His many members. Now in the definition of the universal man, we have a full picture that we as the many members of His mysterious and wonderful Body were originally sinful before God and under His condemnation according to the law. There is no other book or portion of the Scriptures that tells us that we are sinful in the eyes of God as fully as the first three chapters of Romans. I expect that all the young brothers and sisters would spend the time to study this book. We should spend an adequate time to study it because it gives us a full sketch and understanding of the Christian life. It is not too much to spend even one year to study it. We need two or three months just to study the first section alone.

The Knowledge of God, the Conscience of Man, and the Law of God

The first section of Romans tells us something concerning the knowledge of God, the conscience of man, and the law of God. These three matters are the basic points of this section. How can we know that we are sinful? It is by the knowledge of God, by our conscience, and by the law of God. If there were no God in this universe, no knowledge of God, no conscience in human beings, and no law given to us by God, there would be no knowledge of sin. However, because there is a God in this universe, the knowledge of God, a conscience within us, and the law of God outside of us, we cannot escape God's condemnation. Outside of man in the universe there is a just and righteous God, and within man He made a conscience to reflect what He is. Then, at a certain time God gave the law, the commandments, to regulate us. By these regulations we know whether we are wrong or right.

In the first section of Romans there are three parts. Verse 18 of chapter one to the end of the chapter deals with the knowledge of God. By the knowledge of God we are condemned as sinful. The second part is the first half of chapter two, which deals with the conscience. This part deals particularly with the Gentiles because the Gentiles do not have the law of God, but within them they have their conscience (2:14-16). Because of their conscience, the Gentiles cannot say that they are not sinful. Therefore, due to their conscience, which represents God and reflects what He is, they are condemned before God. The third part of the first section of Romans deals with the law of God (2:17—3:8). Strictly speaking, this part deals with the Jews because they are under the law of God. According to the law of God, the Jews also are sinful and condemned.

God's Standard Being God Himself

Concerning whether we are right or wrong, whether we are righteous or sinful, the standard is God Himself. The knowledge of God comes from God Himself, and this knowledge to some extent has been installed into us through our conscience. Human nature has the function of the conscience. The function of the conscience, which is within us, is related to the knowledge of God. Regardless of whether we are a Jew or a Gentile, we all have the function of the conscience within us, reflecting the knowledge of God to some extent, though not in a full way. Then, in order to establish the knowledge of God and make it more definite, God at a certain time gave man the law, which is a better reflection of the knowledge of God.

Therefore, when the apostle Paul was inspired to deal with the sinful human race, the standard he uplifted was God Himself with the knowledge of God, the conscience, and the law. Paul compared all of man's deeds with God Himself, with the knowledge of God, with the conscience, and with the law of God. Therefore, his conclusion to the first main section of Romans is that all humans are shut up by the law; there is no excuse and no escape (3:9-20). Every human being is shut up by the law and is under the condemnation of God.

Keeping the above items and important words clearly in mind, we should again read 1:18—3:20. These items and terms are the open windows, the light, by which we can see clearly. In order to preach the gospel to tell people that they are sinful, we must find the best way to convince and convict them. In principle, we cannot convince people effectively unless we present to them either God Himself with the knowledge of God or the conscience. Many times we must touch the conscience of people in order to convince them that they are sinful. Many prevailing evangelists have preached a great deal about the law of God. They defined the law of God to people for the purpose of convincing them of their sinfulness. If we want to convince unbelievers that they are sinners, we must make God and the knowledge of God very clear to them. We must also learn how to strike their conscience and use the law of God to expose them. Then they will be enlightened and convicted that they are sinners.

We as members of the wonderful universal man were originally sinful persons. In light of the knowledge of God, our human conscience, and the divine law, we were sinful and under God's condemnation. There was absolutely no escape and no possibility for us to do anything that could be justified by God. We must bow ourselves to God and to God's divine law, being convinced by our conscience that we are sinners who need God's redemption. This is the conclusion and the basic point of the first section of Romans. If we receive this word and keep it in mind, we can be crystal clear when we read this portion.

JUSTIFICATION

We have seen that the first section of Romans speaks of the knowledge of God (1:28), the conscience (2:15), and the law of God (v. 17). The best way to study the Word of God is to find the central lines and the main points. If we have the central lines and the main points, everything will be open and crystal clear. Without the main points, however, the more we speak, define, and explain, the more we are not clear. Therefore, just as we have seen the basic points of the first section of Romans, we need the right words to describe the content and insight of the second section. However, this is the most difficult section. After reading from 3:21 to 5:11 many times, we still may not know what this portion of the Word tells us and how to summarize it.

The Glory of God

The second main section of Romans gives us a full picture of how we are justified through the redemption of Christ (3:24). The first basic term in this section is *the glory of God.* Romans 3:23 says, "For all have sinned and fall short of the glory of God." The glory of God is the standard of God's justification. When we human beings measure ourselves against the standard of the glory of God, we realize that God's glory is higher than the heavens. How can we compare with it? When we come to the glory of God, we fall short.

The Righteousness of God

The second main term is *the righteousness of God* (vv. 21-22, 25-26). Only God's righteousness comes up to the standard of God's glory and matches God's glory. No matter how high the standard of God's glory is, God's righteousness reaches that standard; it is just as high as God's glory. Man by himself can never be justified by God because the standard is too high. It is impossible for us to reach that standard. This is the thought in this section.

Propitiation

The third important word is *propitiation* (v. 25). We have seen that only God's righteousness can reach the standard of His glory, but how can God's righteousness, the highest righteousness, be applied to us? It is through propitiation. Romans 3:25 says, "Whom God set forth as a propitiation place." That this verse begins with *whom* indicates that propitiation is Christ Himself. Christ has been set forth by God as a propitiation; the set-forth Christ is the propitiation.

The phrases *propitiation place* and *set forth* are not easy to translate. In his New Translation, J. N. Darby translates *propitiation place* as *mercy-seat*. We must understand this term in view of the background of the Old Testament types. In the ancient times whenever a sinner realized that he was condemned before God, he needed to be redeemed. This was done by bringing a sin offering to the altar. After this sin offering was slain and its blood shed on the altar, the blood was brought by the high priest into the Holy of Holies and sprinkled on the mercy seat, or expiation cover (Lev. 16:14-15). On the mercy seat there was propitiation. By this propitiation and at this propitiation place, a sinner could be forgiven. Here his sins were forgiven, and he was redeemed and made one with God. This is the meaning of propitiation. Romans 3:24-25 tells us that Christ Himself was made such a propitiation place.

God's Setting Forth of Christ

God began to set forth Christ as the propitiation place at the time that darkness came over the whole land during His crucifixion, when He offered Himself as the unique sacrifice for sin, the reality of the sin offering (Luke 23:44; Heb. 9:26). Then, on the third day God resurrected Him; this resurrection was also a part of the process of God's setting forth of Christ. After the Lord's resurrection, God received Christ into the heavens and placed Him at His right hand. This receiving and placing are also a part of the setting forth. God set forth Christ through the entire process of His crucifixion, resurrection, and ascension to sit at the right hand of God. This setting forth makes Christ Himself the very propitiation. Now by Christ as the propitiation, the righteousness of God can be applied to us.

This section of Romans says that on the one hand, we are justified through the redemption in Christ Jesus, that is, through faith in His blood (3:24-25), and on the other hand, we are justified because of the resurrection of Christ (4:25). The shedding of blood and the resurrection of Christ are the main steps in the process of the setting forth of Christ by God. By this means God set forth Christ as a propitiation place. God placed Christ, set forth Christ, from the time that He shed His blood to the time that He ascended to sit at the right hand of God. It is by this propitiation that what God recognizes can be applied to us and become ours. We must never forget that propitiation includes Christ Himself, His crucifixion, His resurrection, and His ascension.

Experiencing Propitiation by Faith

The fourth crucial word in this section of Romans is *faith* (3:25-31). We have seen the glory of God, the righteousness of God, and Christ as the propitiation place. The way to experience propitiation is by faith. These terms are difficult to grasp because they are not found in our human concept.

Reaching God's Standard by Justification

The fifth important word is *justification* (4:25; 3:24, 26). The main thought of justification is that we come up to God's standard. By faith we experience propitiation, and by propitiation God's own righteousness becomes ours. Hence, we can reach the standard of God's glory. Now we are justified and do not fall short.

Being Reconciled to God

After justification we have *reconciliation* (5:10-11). To be reconciled means to have peace and harmony. Now because of justification, we are in harmony with God. Between us and God there is peace and real harmony.

Boasting in God

As we have seen, six main points are found in the second section of Romans: God's glory, God's righteousness, Christ Himself set forth as the propitiation, faith, justification, and reconciliation. The last verse of this section says, "And not only so, but also boasting in God through our Lord Jesus Christ, through whom we have now received the reconciliation" (5:11). Eventually, this entire section brings us into God. In this reconciliation we are enjoying God, boasting in God, and glorying in God. Now God is our portion. We are not only reconciled to God, but by justification we are in God, and God is our boast, our enjoyment, and our everything. This is the conclusion of this section of Romans.

In summary, God's glory is His standard. If we are not up to that standard, we cannot pass the test. It is impossible to measure up to His standard in ourselves, but His righteousness is the potential for us to come up to the standard of His glory. Now His righteousness is ours because God set forth Christ as the propitiation place. The way that we share propitiation is by faith. When we believe in Christ, we share propitiation, and under this propitiation and in this propitiation God's righteousness is ours. Now we have a righteousness that is not our own but God's. Moreover, this righteousness brings us and uplifts us to the standard of God's glory, so we are justified. Because of this justification we are in harmony with God; that is, we are reconciled to God. There is real peace and harmony between us and God. Now we are in God, and we boast, glory, and rejoice in Him. God is our boast, our portion, and our enjoyment. This is the meaning of justification. May we be impressed deeply with these matters.

Romans 5:10 says, "For if we, being enemies, were reconciled to God through the death of His Son, much more we will be saved in His life, having been reconciled." To be saved in His life is dealt with in the following section of Romans, which immediately follows verse 11.

CHAPTER TEN

SANCTIFICATION IN ROMANS

Scripture Reading: Rom. 5:12-21; 6:4-6, 11, 19; 7:1-6, 18,
20-25; 8:2, 4, 6

The third main section of Romans, the middle part, is the
heart of this book. This part of Romans begins from 5:12 and
continues to the end of chapter eight. All Bible students agree
that the things mentioned in this section and the thoughts
contained here are very deep.

THE GIFT IN CHRIST AND THE HERITAGE IN ADAM

In chapter five there are several key words. The first two
are related to two persons. The first person is Adam, and the
second person is Christ (5:14-15). Related to the first person,
Adam, the two key words are *sin* and *death* (vv. 13-14, 21a).
Sin is the cause, and death is the effect. Related to the second
man, Christ, the two key words are *righteousness* and *life*
(vv. 17-19, 21b). Righteousness is the cause, and life is the
effect. Therefore, righteousness is versus sin, and life is
versus death. We inherit sin and death from the first man,
but we receive righteousness and life in Christ, the second
man (v. 17). All the things in Adam were inherited by us,
whereas all the benefits in Christ are received by us. Therefore, the key items in chapter five are Adam, Christ, sin,
death, righteousness, life, inheriting, and receiving.

IDENTIFICATION WITH CHRIST

In Romans 6, the most important term is the word *grown*.
Verse 5 says, "We have grown together with Him." *Grown* is a
difficult word to translate. There are several translations of
this word, including *grafted,* as a branch grafted from one tree

onto another. The King James Version translates it as *planted,* the American Standard Version as *united,* and J. N. Darby's New Translation as *identified.* Another translation renders this word as *joined* and another as *incorporated.* Therefore, there are at least these different renderings of this one word: *grown, planted, grafted, united, identified, joined,* and *incorporated.* Of these, *grafted* and *identified* are two of the better translations. This is the most important term in this entire chapter. We are grafted into Christ and identified with Him. Christ and we, we and Christ, are one in this grafting, in this identification. We are no more two; we are one with Christ.

There are a number of other key words in this section: *crucified, buried,* and *resurrection* (vv. 4-6). Since we are identified with Christ and one with Him, in Him we are crucified, buried, and resurrected. We are identified with Him especially in His crucifixion, in His burial, and in His resurrection.

Some other important terms found here are the *old man* and *newness of life* (vv. 4, 6). We must keep all these key terms in mind; otherwise, we will not be able to understand this section. The old man has been crucified and buried in order that we may walk in newness of life. Our walk must be in newness of life; once we are identified with Christ in His death, burial, and resurrection, we no longer live by the old man but walk in newness of life.

To complete this section, we must add the key words *reckon* and *present* (vv. 11, 19). When we realize that we are one with Christ, we reckon that His death is our death in Him and that when He was buried and resurrected, we were buried and resurrected in Him also. In such an identification, we simply reckon that we are dead to sin but living to God. Then in verse 19 Paul says, "Present your members as slaves to righteousness unto sanctification." Based on our reckoning that we are dead to sin and alive to God, we present our members as slaves to righteousness.

These nine key terms—*grafted, identified, crucifixion, burial, resurrection, old man, newness of life, reckoning,* and *presenting*—make the entire picture of Romans 6 very clear to us.

In chapter five we are told that we were born in Adam, but now we have been transferred out of Adam into Christ. In Adam we inherited sin and death, but now in Christ we receive righteousness, which is versus sin, and life, which is versus death. However, in order for us to understand how we are transferred into Christ, we need the definition and explanation in chapter six. We are transferred out of Adam and into Christ by identification. We are identified with Him, that is, planted, grafted, and united with Him. Therefore, His death becomes ours, His burial becomes ours, and His resurrection also becomes ours. In other words, His experience is our history. In this way, our old man has been crucified and we are now walking in newness of life, which is the newness of Christ Himself. Therefore, we must reckon ourselves dead to sin and alive to God. For this purpose we must present ourselves, especially all the members of our body, no longer to sin but to righteousness.

BONDAGE IN THE FLESH BY THE INDWELLING SIN

The Law of God

Although it is somewhat easy for us to understand chapter six, it is not easy to understand chapter seven. It is a "hard hill to climb." Even many Bible students do not understand chapter seven correctly. There are several key terms found in this chapter. The first important term is *the law of God,* that is, the Ten Commandments with all of its supplements (vv. 22, 7, 10). This is the law given by Moses.

The Flesh

The second key word is *flesh.* Paul said, "For I know that in me, that is, in my flesh, nothing good dwells" (v. 18). Whereas chapter six speaks of the old man, chapter seven deals with the flesh. In the Scriptures the word *flesh* has at least three meanings. In a positive sense it refers to the flesh, bone, and blood as a part of our physical body, the element and constituent of our body. Second, the flesh is the corrupted body. This is on the negative side. Although God had created a body for us which was upright and pure, it was poisoned by Satan. It was corrupted by the fruit of the tree of the knowledge of good and evil. Our body, created by God and clean in nature, was corrupted and degraded to become the flesh.

Third, in the Scriptures the flesh is the completely fallen man (3:20; Gal. 1:16). Man has fallen to such an extent that he is absolutely under the control and influence of the flesh. Therefore, the Scriptures tell us that the fallen man is called *flesh*. This is mentioned clearly in Genesis 6:3 and 12-13. *All flesh* in these verses indicates that fallen man lives under the control of the flesh, so in the eyes of God he has become flesh. In Romans 7 the word *flesh* implies the entire fallen man, including his spirit and soul, under the control of the flesh, but the primary meaning is the corrupted body.

The flesh is the living out of the old man. Before the life of the old man is lived out, it is simply the old man, but once it is lived out, it is the flesh. Regardless of how nice someone is, he is still the old man, but we do not realize he is the old man until we see the flesh, that is, his entire living, action, walk, and attitude. The old man in chapter six is expressed and lived out as the flesh in chapter seven. The flesh in doctrine is the old man, and the old man in experience is the flesh.

The flesh is the old man in testimony, living, and moving. In chapter six the old man is there in position only, not in action, but in chapter seven there is the old man in action, so he becomes the flesh. The old man there is very active, living, and moving, especially in striving to do good and to overcome evil. Therefore, he is the flesh.

The Law in the Members of Our Body

The third main point in Romans 7 is the law in our members. The first law in chapter seven is the law of Moses; the second law, the law in the members of our body, is an evil law. In chapter eight it is called the law of sin and of death (v. 2). This law in the members of our physical body is, no doubt, something of the satanic life. Due to the fall, when man partook of the tree of the knowledge of good and evil, the satanic life was injected into the human body. The fruit of the tree of knowledge was taken into man's body, so his body was poisoned. Therefore, in the human body there is something evil. According to the revelation of the Scriptures, all of our doing that issues from the tree of knowledge is something related to sin. When man took of the fruit of the tree of knowledge and ate it, the evil element of Satan entered into his body. This corresponds with the thought in Romans 7 that there is a law in our members. Since God did not create this law of sin in the members of the human body, it must be something from the fruit of the tree of knowledge which was taken into man's body and which is something of Satan. Therefore, this law of evil, the law of sin and death, is something of the satanic life.

The principle of any law is that it always corresponds with its life. With a certain kind of life, there is a certain kind of law. For example, there is no need to teach a cat how to catch a mouse. Within the cat's life there is a law to catch mice. In the same way, there is no need to teach a dog to bark; within the dog's life is a law to bark. With the vegetable life, there are also laws. The cauliflower is a plant whose law produces white leaves. Another kind of plant has its own law that brings forth yellow leaves. Similarly, there is no need to teach flowers to bloom. There is a blossoming law in their life.

In the same way, we have the law of sin and death in our members because we have the satanic life within us. This can be proven by the fact that unbelievers are called the children of the devil. First John 3:9-10 says that a man who practices sin is a child of the devil, and in John 8:44 the Lord Jesus told the evil Pharisees that their father was the devil.

The Law of the Mind

There is yet another law, the third law, which is the law of the mind. Romans 7:23 says, "But I see a different law in my members, warring against the law of my mind." We should not consider that the law of the mind is the same as the law of God given through Moses. The Mosaic law is outside of us, whereas the law of the mind is within us. Because the mind is a part of the soul, the law of the mind is the law in our soul. The two laws in verse 23 are subjective laws, not the objective law. One is subjectively in the members of our body, and the other is subjectively in our mind. These two laws, one in our members and the other in our mind, war against one another.

As we have seen, with every kind of life there is a corresponding law. Since the human life in our soul was created by God, it is good. Therefore, the law of this life must also be good. Since this created life is in the soul, the law of good is in the soul. Therefore, it is called the law of the mind because the mind is a part of the soul. This law of good in our mind, the law of the good life, corresponds with the law of God. When the law of God outside of us demands that we do something good, the law in our mind always responds. However, whenever the law of the mind responds to the law of God in trying to do good, the law in our members rises up to frustrate and war against the law of the mind. The law of God and the law in the mind "love" one another, but they can never "marry" because the law in our members is the enemy that frustrates them by warring against the law in the mind.

The warring in Romans 7 pertains to unbelievers as well as to believers, because in Romans 7 there is nothing yet related to salvation. In God's creation we obtained the created human life in our soul. Within this created life, which is good, there is the law of good. When man fell, however, he received the life of Satan into his body. Within this evil life there is the law of evil which is the law of sin and death dwelling in the members of man's body.

If you have ever seen opium smokers, you will be very clear about this matter. I saw them when I was young. In their mind the opium smokers were convinced that they should not smoke, and they made up their mind never to smoke. However, after a few hours the drug addiction in their body would rise up. They could not stand against that addiction. There was a law in their members, the law of addiction. No matter how hard they struggled against this addiction, they eventually were carried away captive to the smoking house. Paul said, "But I see a different law in my members, warring against the law of my mind and making me a captive to the law of sin which is in my members" (v. 23). Even an opium smoker realizes that there is something in his members that wars against something in his mind and carries him away as a captive to the law of addiction in his members. All manner of lusts are also addictions in the members of the body. Therefore, the Scriptures tell us that lusts are related to the flesh.

Released from the Bondage of Sin
and from the Obligation of the Law

We have now mentioned four important terms—*the law of God, the flesh, the law in the members,* and *the law of the mind.* We must also remember the word *warring.* There is warfare between the law in the members and the law of the mind. A sixth crucial term in Romans 7 is the word *dead.* We are dead to the law (v. 4). While we are still alive, we are obligated to the law, but when we are dead, we are liberated; we have no more obligations.

In Romans 7:1-6 Paul speaks of the law regarding the husband, and we are likened to a wife. After a woman marries, she is obligated to her husband; she has no liberty. When the husband dies, however, the wife is liberated. The interpretation of the husband in Romans 7 is a great problem. There have been many debates concerning who the husband is. Some say that the husband refers to the law, but how can the law die (v. 3)?

Verses 1-6 say, "Or are you ignorant, brothers (for I speak to those who know the law), that the law lords it over the man as long as he lives? For the married woman is bound by the law to her husband while he is living; but if the husband dies, she is discharged from the law regarding the husband. So then if, while the husband is living, she is joined to another man, she will be called an adulteress; but if the husband dies, she is free from the law, so that she is not an adulteress, though she is joined to another man. So then, my brothers, you also have been made dead to the law through the body of Christ so that you might be joined to another, to Him who has been raised from the dead, that we might bear fruit to God. For when we were in the flesh, the passions for sins, which acted through the law, operated in our members to bear fruit to death. But now we have been discharged from the law, having died to that in which we were held, so that we serve in newness of spirit and not in oldness of letter."

In these verses the husband, not the wife, dies, and the wife is released from the law of the husband. Some may interpret this to say that we have no obligation toward the old man as a husband, that rather we are obligated to the law. If this is so, then the husband is the law. However, there is a problem with this interpretation because these verses say that the husband dies. Since the law cannot die, it must be the old man that has died (6:6). From 1925 to 1927, I spent a great deal of time to study this matter. In the first letter I wrote to Watchman Nee I asked him who the husband is in Romans 7. In his reply, he said that on the one hand, the husband is the old man, but on the other hand, the husband involves the law. This is because the old man and the law are very related to one another.

On the one hand, we are the old man, while on the other hand, the old man is something we have. For this reason, Romans 6:6 uses the phrase *our old man*. When we were in the old man, we were obligated to the law of God. However, our old man has been crucified, so we are now released from the law. From this point of view, the husband is the old man, who is subject to the law, and we are the wife of the old man. While our old man is living, we as the wife of the old man are obligated to the law, but now that the old man as our husband has died, we are released from the obligation of the law.

The most important point in chapter seven is that our old man, that is, we as the old man, are dead in Christ. Therefore, we have nothing to do with the law. Hence, we should not try to keep the law anymore. We have no more obligation to it because the old man is dead and we are released. Chapter six tells us that we are dead in Christ, so we are released from sin (vv. 6, 11, 18, 22), while chapter seven also says that we are dead; here, however, it says that we are released from the law. In chapter six we are released from sin, while in chapter seven we are released from the law, both by our death with Christ. When we died with Christ, we were released from sin, and we were also released from the law. While we were living in the old man, we were under the bondage of sin, and at the same time we were under the obligation of the law. Now we are released from the bondage of sin and from the obligation of the law.

These are the most important matters in this section, but in these few chapters nearly every word is a key word. Chapter six speaks of the body of sin (v. 6), and chapter seven speaks of the body of death (v. 24). The physical body spoken of in chapter six is a body of sin, which in chapter seven is called the body of death. The body of sin is very active and powerful to commit sin, but in doing the will of God and in keeping the law, it is a body of death; it is inactive, powerless, and weak to the uttermost.

In chapters six and seven there is another important term, which is personified Sin. Romans 6:14 says that sin lords it over us, and 7:17 says that sin dwells in us. The apostle Paul says, "But if what I do not will, this I do, it is no longer I that work it out but sin that dwells in me" (v. 20). Sin, therefore, is something living, moving, acting, and doing things within us and through us, indicating that it is alive.

THE LAW OF THE SPIRIT OF LIFE

Freedom in the Spirit
by the Highest and Strongest Law

In Romans 8 there is a wonderful term: *the law of the Spirit of life* (v. 2). In this phrase three things are composed together: law, Spirit, and life. This law is the fourth law that Paul mentions in Romans. In chapter seven there are three laws: the law of God, the law in our members, and the law of the mind. The law of the Spirit of life, no doubt, is the law of the divine life. By regeneration we received the divine life into our spirit, and with this highest life, there is the highest law. This law liberates us from the law of sin and death.

As we have seen, the third law, that is, the law of the mind, always responds and corresponds to the first law, the law of God. The problem, however, is with the second law, the law of sin and death. Because the third law is weaker than the second law, the second law always defeats the third law and brings us into captivity. However, the fourth law, the law of the Spirit of life, is the highest and strongest law, which liberates us from the second law and fulfills all the requirements of the first law. This is clearly mentioned in Romans 8:2 and 4.

The Mind Set on the Flesh or on the Spirit

Verse 6 is another very important verse in Romans 8. Nearly every word in it is a key, because it is related to the three lives and four laws. As we have seen, the first law, the law of God, is outside of us and above us. The other three laws are all within us. The second law, the law of sin and death, is in our members. The third law, the law of our mind, is in our mind. The fourth law, the law of the Spirit of life, is in our spirit. This corresponds to the three parts—body, soul, and spirit—of our created, fallen, and regenerated person. In each part of our being there is a law. In our body there is the law of the satanic life, in our soul is the law of the human life, and in our spirit there is the law of the divine life. After God's creation of man and before man's fall, there was only one life in man with two laws. Although the law of God at that time was not given yet, it was there already in principle. Man had the created human life with the law of good within him to do the things which corresponded with God's demand, that is, God's law.

After the fall, however, a second life came in, and with this life there is an evil law. At this point, the trouble within man began. The law of God makes a demand, and the law of good within our soul, our human life, always tries to respond to God's law. Because our mind is fallen, however, it does not always stand on the side of good, the side of the law of God. When our mind does not stand with the side of good, the second law will not rise up. However, whenever our mind sides with the side of good, the second law, the law of sin and death, comes in to interrupt and frustrate us. The law of the satanic life frustrates us and wars against the law in the human mind. This satanic law is stronger than the law of our human life. So, the human life with the law of the human life is always defeated. However, at the time of regeneration, we received the strongest life with the strongest law. This law, which is the law of the Spirit of life, can now deliver us. This law sets us free from the law of sin, fulfills the requirements of the law of God, and satisfies the desire of the law of the human life.

The operation of the law of these lives depends on which side the mind takes. The mind can side with the flesh, which has the law of sin in our members, or it can side with the spirit, with the law of the divine life in our spirit. There are two sides, and the mind is in the middle. Our experience depends on what side our mind stands with. Romans 8:6 says, "For the mind set on the flesh is death, but the mind set on the spirit is life and peace." Three things are mentioned in verse 6. The flesh is outside, the spirit is inside, and the mind is in the middle representing the soul. Now the mind can stand with the flesh on the outside or the spirit within. For our mind to stand with the flesh brings in death, but if our mind stands with the spirit, we will have life and peace. If we are not clear about this, it will be difficult for us to have real experiences of the Lord.

Because we were created, became fallen, and then were regenerated, the same mind on one occasion can be good and on another occasion not good. Romans 7:22 clearly indicates that the mind delights in the law of God, and verse 25 says, "So then with the mind I myself serve the law of God." This means that the law of good in our mind always corresponds to the law of God, but this does not mean that the fallen mind is absolutely good. Other passages in the New Testament tell us that the mind is sinful and evil, such as Ephesians 2:3, which says, "We also all conducted ourselves once in the lusts of our flesh, doing the desires of the flesh and of the thoughts." The mind in Romans 7:25 is mentioned in a good sense. The mind of the spirit in Romans 8:6, however, is the mind set on the spirit.

CHAPTER ELEVEN

SANCTIFICATION, GLORIFICATION, SELECTION, AND THE BODY LIFE IN ROMANS

Scripture Reading: Rom. 8:6, 4, 14, 28-30, 32, 35, 38-39; 9:16; 11:5; 12:1-2, 11, 4-5

SANCTIFICATION

Three Parties with Three Wills, Three Lives, and Three Laws

As we saw in the previous chapter, Romans 7 and 8 speak of three lives and four laws. The law of God, that is, the law of letters, is outside of man, demanding us to do good and to do the will of God according to what God is. The other three laws are within us subjectively. In each part of man as a tripartite being there is a law. In our body is the law of sin, in our soul is the law of good, and in our spirit is the law of life. Our thought may be that the goal is merely to do good. However, God's intention for man is not merely that we do good but that we live by His life, that is, by Him as life.

We must remember well that in this universe there are three parties—God, Satan, and man. With these three parties there are three wills—the divine will of God, the devilish will of Satan, and the human will of man. From the Scriptures it is easy to realize that the devilish will is always struggling to frustrate the divine will; Satan's will always tries to damage and hinder God's will. Therefore, in the universe there is a battle raging. Even science tells us that there is something contradictory in the universe, like a battle, a warfare. This is because there are two wills—the divine will and the satanic will—contradicting one another and fighting against one another.

In addition, God created a third will, that is, the human will. God created this will with the intention that this will would stand with Him. However, God did not force the human will to stand with Him; God gave man a free choice, his own volition. Therefore, this will can choose either side. If man so desires, he can choose God. However, if he likes, he can also choose to stand with Satan. If man chooses God and stands with God's will, God can then accomplish His purpose. However, if man chooses to stand with Satan, then Satan can do something to frustrate God's will. Therefore, there are three parties and three wills.

With each will there is a particular life. Just as there is the divine life with the divine will and the satanic life with the devilish will, there is the human life with the human will. Moreover, with each life there is an accompanying law. We do not say that a life is a law; rather, with any kind of life there is a law. According to biologists, it is a scientific fact that with any kind of physical life, there are principles and laws. With the divine life there is also the divine law, with the satanic life there is the satanic law, and with the human life there is the human law. In short, there are three wills with their respective lives, and each of these lives has its own law. Always remember these three things.

The Three Parties in the Garden of Eden

At the very beginning of the Scriptures there are these three parties in the garden of Eden. Adam stood in front of two trees, which represent or symbolize two parties—God and Satan. The tree of life represented God, Adam was there representing man, and Satan was there as well represented by the tree of knowledge. This clear picture shows us that both God and Satan became a choice to man. God Himself was there with Satan in front of man, and God gave man a volition to allow him to make a choice. Therefore, in the garden there are three parties, three wills, three lives, and three laws.

In the garden these three parties were individual and separated. God was God, Satan was Satan, and man was man; none of these three were mingled with the others. God's intention was that man would receive Him as life. However, before man received God into him, Satan took the first step; he did something first. Man was seduced to take in Satan, Satan entered into man, and the two—man and Satan, Satan and man—were joined together illegally. Hence, Satan is within man as well as outside of him.

Some may feel that it is too much to say that Satan is in us. However, Ephesians 2:2 says, "You once walked according to the age of this world, according to the ruler of the authority of the air, of the spirit which is now operating in the sons of disobedience." Satan, the ruler of the authority of the air, is working in man. This is a proof that Satan is in fallen man. When did Satan enter into man? It was at the time that Adam took the fruit of the tree of knowledge. This is why the Bible tells us that fallen men are called the children of the devil and that Satan is the father of sinful man (1 John 3:10; John 8:44). When Satan entered into man, the satanic law of his evil life came with him.

In God's salvation, He not only redeemed us, but also regenerated us. Redemption is a matter of the Lord shedding His blood, while regeneration is a matter of life. In God's salvation there is not only the wonderful blood but also a wonderful life. On the negative side, blood is for redemption, while on the positive side, the divine life is for regeneration. Blood represents what the Lord has done for us, His work. Life represents what the Lord is to us, the Lord's person. We believe in the Lord's redemptive work by the blood, and we believe in His person as life to us. When we believe into Him in this way, we are redeemed on the negative side, and we are regenerated on the positive side. This means that our sins are forgiven, and we receive Him as life. In this way, He comes into us.

It is not difficult to prove in what part Satan came into us. Satan came into our physical body, because at the time of the fall Adam ate of the fruit of the tree of knowledge with his body and took it into his body. It is even less difficult to prove in what part the Lord came into us. We all know that the Lord comes into our human spirit (1 Cor. 6:17; Rom. 8:16). In addition to these two lives, the human life is in the soul. Now we can see the site of each of the three different lives within us.

The body is the site of the satanic life, the soul is the site of the human life, and the spirit is the site of the divine life. This is why Romans 7 and 8 tell us clearly that in the members of our body there is the law of sin, in the mind of the soul there is the law of good, and in the spirit there is the law of the divine life. Nothing could be clearer than this.

The Garden of Eden within Us

The problem that we Christians face today is that there is a garden of Eden within us. All three parties were not only in the garden, but they now are in us, making us a miniature garden of Eden. In the ancient time there were three parties in the garden of Eden, and today the same parties are all within us. Within us there is the human life with the human will and the law of good. Within us there is also the satanic life with the satanic will and the satanic law. Furthermore, within us there is the divine life with the divine will and the divine law. Therefore, our story is the same as Adam's. Even as God gave Adam a free will, a volition, to choose, He gives us the same volition and will with a choice.

If we want to go along with Satan, there is no need for us to go far away. If we choose to make friends with Satan, there is no need for a telephone call; he is close to us, even within us. Wherever we go, he always accompanies us; he never leaves us. Never think that Satan has ever left us. If we say this, we are deceived. The evil life of Satan is still in our members. One day Peter said something good to the Lord. However, he himself was not aware that Satan was in him. Therefore, the Lord turned and said to Peter, "Get behind Me, Satan!" (Matt. 16:23). Although we do not say that Satan is omnipresent, we must realize that he dwells in man's flesh; this is a fact according to the Scriptures. Today Satan, the evil spirit, is working in mankind. As long as we are human beings, we are still in this fallen body, so we must be aware that the evil life with the evil law is still in us. However, although this evil thing is in our body, we still must praise and thank God that the divine life is in our spirit.

Since we are still in the body, we are very much related to the evil things. This is why we must daily and hourly rely on the Lord's blood when we come to contact Him. Whether or not we sense that we are sinful or wrong, we still need the blood. In the Old Testament type, no one could go into the presence of the Lord without the shedding of blood. Whether we feel that we are sinful or holy, we still need the blood because we are still in this sinful body, the body of sin. Yet, we must praise the Lord because He also is in us! He is in us in an even deeper way.

The Secret of Setting Our Mind on the Spirit

Satan dwells in the members of our body, but God is in our spirit. This brings us to Romans 8:6. This verse contains a real secret. In this verse there are three things: the mind, the flesh, and the spirit. It says, "For the mind set on the flesh is death, but the mind set on the spirit is life and peace." I have studied many translations of this verse, and this is the one that is the most correct according to the meaning of the original Greek. The translations in the New American Standard Bible and the Revised Standard Version are also good and convey the same meaning.

In this verse we again see the three parties. We human beings are represented by the mind, and Satan, the evil one, is in the flesh. The spirit here is the mingling of two spirits—the divine Spirit and the human spirit. It is rather difficult to tell whether *spirit* in Romans 8 is the Holy Spirit or the human spirit. In verse 6 it refers to the two spirits mingled as one. This can be proved by verse 16 which says, "The Spirit Himself witnesses with our spirit." Therefore, in the spirit there is God, the divine One, in the mind there is man, and in the flesh there is Satan.

Now our experience depends on whom or what we would set ourselves, that is, our mind. If we set our mind on the flesh, that is, on Satan, the issue is death. Adam did this when he partook of the fruit of the tree of knowledge, with the same result of death. However, if we set our mind on God as life, the result is life and peace. As Christians today there is no need for us to try to overcome the flesh, and there is no need to try to defeat the law of sin; we cannot do that. What we need to do is simply stand with the Spirit and rely upon

Him. What we need is the deliverance in the spirit. We must stand with the spirit, set our mind on the spirit, and rely upon the Lord. Then we will be delivered.

This is the secret that we all must learn. After being a Christian for many years, I believe that no other teachings are so necessary as this teaching. Of course, the teachings concerning the Lord Himself, who the Lord is, what the Lord is, and what the Lord has done for us are very necessary. Subjectively speaking, however, the teaching of Romans 8:6 is the most necessary. We may illustrate this with driving a car. There are many things involved with driving a car, but the most important thing is to be aware of what is immediately around us. If we know this, we can drive enjoyably and without effort. There is no need to push or pull the car, and there is no need for us to run, walk, or use much energy. We simply can sit there and enjoy our driving, because it is not we who are running, but the car.

However, we must learn the secret of cooperating with the car. Whether or not the car runs depends on us. Today we have the "car," but we must know how to "drive" it. If we know how, there is no problem, and there is no need of our energy. Thirty-five years ago I was still struggling, but praise Him, today I have no struggle! I know that my spirit is my "car," and I know how to "drive" it. Today, even a person who is crippled can drive a car, because it is not he who carries the car but the car that carries him. However, the car needs him to drive it. In the same way, it is not we who defeat the enemy; it is the divine life that carries us to gain the victory, but the divine life needs us to "drive" it.

The secret is not found even in Romans 6:6 or 6:11; the secret is found in Romans 8:6. We must learn how to set our mind on the spirit. In other words, we must learn to trust in God and depend on the Lord. If we know how to rely on the Lord and trust in Him, and if we do it, everything will be all right. This can be illustrated by the use of electric appliances. All we have to know is how to plug them in. There is no trouble unless we do not plug them in; in that case, no one can help us. If we desire and know how to handle the appliances, then we can plug them in whenever we need them. This is simple, yet it is a secret that we all must learn.

I stress these matters because I do not have the burden to give you mere doctrine. If there is a need for us to learn doctrine, it is solely for the purpose to "drive the car." Our knowledge and understanding of the construction of a car and the arrangement of its parts is for one purpose—to drive it. To be familiar with the parts of the car and the operation of the engine helps, but that is not the secret. The secret is the driving. Similarly, although we must study the Bible with its narratives and instructions, the real secret is in Romans 8:6. We may be very knowledgeable of the Scriptures, but if we do not apply Romans 8:6, whatever we know and do will accomplish little.

Day and night for many years I have been studying the Bible. I have not found another verse as important as Romans 8:6 as far as our spiritual experience is concerned. The way to "drive" in our spiritual experience is in this verse. Now that I have presented many things to you from Romans, beginning from chapter one up to chapter eight, we come to 8:6. This is the very place and the secret for us to know how to "drive the car."

Within us there are three wills, three lives, and three laws. We ourselves are here, Satan is in us, and God is in us. Now we must pray, "Lord, help me to choose You. Help me to rely on You, depend on You, and drop my effort and striving. Help me never to do anything by myself to overcome evil or temptation. Rather, help me always to rely on You, stand with You, and trust in You. Lord, I would never do anything to try to correct myself or deliver myself. Lord, help me always to thrust myself upon You, trust in You, and depend on You."

Such an experience of depending on the Lord is sweet and very available. Its availability may be compared to the electricity in homes. In our homes electricity is so available. Likewise, we should "plug" into the Lord right away, because He is so available. Just as electricity is installed in a house, even in the innermost and hidden chambers of the house, the Lord has been installed in our innermost part. Although this divine electricity is so available, there is one thing that is needed: We need to learn the secret and pray that the Lord would give us the willingness to apply it. We always must be willing to apply it and "plug ourselves in." Although we may listen to hundreds of messages, they may all miss what the real secret of our Christian life is. We have to practice to set our mind on the spirit and to live in this reality all the time.

Walking according to the Spirit by the Inner Anointing

Romans 8:4 tells us to walk according to the spirit. To walk according to the spirit means to go along with the spirit. How can we know the spirit? It is by the sense of life and peace. To understand the sense of life is rather difficult, but to say something about the sense of peace is easier. Whatever we do, we must check within us whether or not we have the peace. Of course, this peace is not an outward peace but an inward peace. Do we have the inner peace or not?

This peace is the issue and result of the inner anointing. When we set our mind on the spirit, the Spirit moves and works within us. If we go along with the anointing, we will feel peaceful, comfortable, and very much in the light. We will be refreshed, strengthened, and satisfied. This is the anointing, and this is the sense of life. We should simply follow this consciousness within. To follow this inner sense, this inner consciousness, means that we are walking according to the spirit.

How do we know that we have life? We are refreshed, strengthened, energized, and satisfied within. Similarly, we know that we have peace because we are at ease and in the light. When we feel empty and darkened within and when we sense a lack of inner peace and comfort, this means that we are not walking according to the spirit. However, when we walk according to the spirit, within us we are always refreshed, satisfied, and strengthened. We continually experience life, peace, and comfort. This means that we are following the Spirit.

Being Led by the Spirit

Romans 8 uses another term—*led by the Spirit*. Verse 14 says, "For as many as are led by the Spirit of God, these are sons of God." Even though *led* is a small word of three letters, it is very important. When we set our mind on the spirit and walk according to the spirit, we are constantly led by the Spirit. In this way we live the life of the genuine sons of God. We are sons of God not only in life and nature but also in daily walk. In daily walk and in everything we are led by the Holy Spirit, and we cooperate with Him in every way.

Being Conformed to the Image of the Son of God

Following this, Romans 8:29 speaks of being conformed to the image of God's Son. By walking according to the spirit, we are progressively conformed to the image of Christ. This is a progression; it is not something accomplished once for all. This is a work that lasts our entire life. The more we walk according to the spirit, the more we are conformed to the image of Christ. This is God's intention. God's intention is to conform us to the image of His Son, that is, to make His Son the Firstborn among many brothers. His intention is to reproduce many sons by and with His Son as the model, the form. Therefore, we must be conformed to the very form, the very image, of Christ.

Day by day, little by little, and part by part the Holy Spirit progressively conforms us to the image of Christ. Verse 28 says, "All things work together for good." This is for the purpose to conform us to the image of Christ. For our conformation we need the Holy Spirit within and "all things" outside of us. This may be compared to baking a cake. To bake a cake, we need the batter within, and we need the heat from the outside. The "batter" on the inside is the Holy Spirit, and the "heat" on the outside is "all things."

Romans 8 has two sections. In the first half there is the Spirit working within, and in the second half, the "all things" work together for good without. All things include sufferings, tribulation, anguish, persecution, famine, nakedness, peril, sword, death, life, angels, principalities, things present, things to come, powers, and so forth (vv. 35, 38). Even our dear wife and children are included in the all things. We praise God that these all things are under His sovereign hand. His sovereign hand is working to arrange all necessary things for our good. This is for the purpose of conforming us to the image of Christ, that is, to produce many brothers for Christ as sons of God so that the only begotten Son might become the Firstborn among many brothers.

GLORIFICATION

The last key word in Romans 8 is *glorified* (v. 30). We are currently in the process of conformation, but our aim is that one day when He returns He will glorify us; He will bring us into glory. This glory is already within us today. One day it will shine out of us in full and swallow up the death in our body. Our body will change in form from a body of humiliation to a body of glory (Phil. 3:21). This is the meaning of glorification.

Although today the glory is within us already, it needs to shine out. It has not yet shined out in full. From the center, the hub, to the rim of our being, this glory is continually expanding, permeating, and saturating our soul to the point that we await only one thing—the Lord's coming. When He returns, this glory will saturate our entire body. At this point our entire body will be changed from a form of humiliation into a glorious form. This is the glorification spoken of in Romans 8.

We can never exhaust the study of this chapter. I have come back to it many times, and it is well-marked in my Bible. The more we read, study, and enter into this chapter, the more glorious it is. In this one portion we can realize the three laws within us, the law of the Spirit of life, and the indwelling Spirit working within us. In addition, there are the "all things" working together for our good to conform us to the image of Christ. This is not simply a matter of overcoming sin, helping us to do good, or fulfilling the requirements of the law; God desires to conform us to the image of His Son. Nothing less than conforming us to the image of Christ will please God. Therefore, we need to be conformed to His image.

We may not have much realization of this truth. We are often troubled that we are weak, defeated, and sinful and that we cannot do good or overcome our weak points. This is largely what we hold in our concept. However, this is not related to God's intention. His intention is much higher. God's intention is to conform us to the image of Christ. It is not a matter of doing good. It is not a matter of defeating the enemy or overcoming our weaknesses. It is a matter of being conformed to the image of Christ. This is much higher and more positive.

It is impossible for us to do this kind of work. There is no potential for this in ourselves, but we praise the Lord that the potential is in Him. He is the Spirit within us, and His sovereign hand is arranging all the necessary things to work together for us. Therefore, we must trust Him. We must entrust ourselves to Him, leave it to Him, and enjoy His working. I say again, it is not simply a matter of doing good, overcoming sin, or defeating the enemy, but to have the very living image of Christ. God will work this out. What we need to do is to cooperate with Him and go along with Him without complaining or murmuring. Whatever happens to us, we praise the Lord, because it is for good. We should always have the assurance that whatever happens to us is measured to us under His sovereign hand. It is in His hand. Then, one day He will come, and we will be in His glorification.

THE SELECTION OF GRACE

Chapters nine, ten, and eleven of Romans can be summed up in one phrase, *the selection of grace* (11:5). Without these three chapters, we may think that believing in the Lord Jesus is something initiated by us. However, after reading these chapters, we realize that it is not we who initiated it; it is God. God elected us, that is, He selected us. Because He selected us in eternity past, we now can believe in Him. The very fact that we are breathing now is a proof that He has selected us. Moreover, this selection can never be changed. It is a selection of God's grace, not a choosing according to our human work or deeds. Therefore, in this section of Romans the most important verse is 9:16, which says, "So then it is not of him who wills, nor of him who runs, but of God who shows mercy." It is not of us who work and struggle but of God who shows mercy and grace.

THE PRACTICE OF THE BODY LIFE

The last main section of Romans is chapters twelve through sixteen. Why do we have to be regenerated and conformed to Christ's image? It is to make us the members of the Body of Christ. All of the items mentioned in the first eight chapters plus the selection of grace in the following three chapters are for the purpose to have a Body for Christ.

The last section of this book is the section of the Body life. If we read these five chapters carefully, it may seem that only chapter thirteen has a little to say about the Body life; however, something more follows concerning the Body. Chapters fourteen and fifteen tell us especially how to receive one another as members; this is something for the Body life. Furthermore, the last part of chapter fifteen tells us how to take care of the needs of other members, how to communicate and contribute something to supply the needs of the members in other parts of the earth; this is also a part of the Body life. Although the last chapter, Romans 16, may appear to have little to do with the Body life, it is full of the Body life. The entire chapter displays the real and practical Body life.

Presenting Our Bodies

In this last section of Romans, there are a number of important terms. First, we must present our bodies (12:1). This is not only a consecration of our mind, will, intention, and heart but a consecration of our bodies. It is to present our bodies as a living sacrifice. There are two bodies mentioned in this chapter. When we present our bodies, we realize the Body of Christ. If we love our body, then His Body, the church, suffers. However, if we present our bodies as a sacrifice, His Body will be built up. We must offer our bodies for His Body's sake. For the church life, the Body life, there is the need of a bodily consecration. We should offer ourselves definitely, materially, and bodily to the Lord. However, if we preserve our bodies for ourselves, then His Body will suffer. In order to build up and care for His Body, we must give our body over to Him by presenting our body.

Being Transformed in Our Soul
by the Renewing of Our Mind

The second matter mentioned in this section is transformation by the renewing of the mind (v. 2). This is something involving our soul. First we need to present our body, and second our soul must be transformed. The mind is a part of the soul. Regeneration has already been accomplished in our spirit, the center of our being, but what we need now is for our soul to be transformed. The Spirit, who is indwelling our spirit, is saturating the part of our being surrounding our spirit as the center in order to transform the soul.

The three parts of man—body, soul, and spirit—are involved here. First, when we practice the church life, the first step that we must take is to present our bodies. However, this is not all. After we present our bodies, our soul needs to be dealt with, so the second thing that we should do is to allow our soul to be transformed. Our mind, our thoughts, and our way of thinking especially have to be transformed. Otherwise, we will not be able to understand what the church life is, and we may even damage the church life. The presenting of our bodies and the transformation of our soul, especially the mind, are the necessary steps for us to practice the Body life.

Being Burning in Spirit
for Our Function in the Church Life

In addition, our spirit must be burning (v. 11). Here we have the body, the soul, and the spirit. We must present our bodies, be transformed in our soul, and learn how to be fervent, that is, burning in spirit in order to function. By practicing these three steps, we have the real, practical experience of the Body life, the church life. The church life depends on our presenting our bodies in a definite way. It also depends on our being transformed in our soul by the renewing of the mind in order to understand God's will in the entire universe, which is to have the church, the Body. In addition, it also depends on our being burning in our spirit to function as a member of His Body. If we do these things, then we will be in the practical experience of the Body life.

For the church life we need to present our bodies, be transformed in our soul, and be burning in spirit for our function in the Body. Our function is an important matter in Romans 12. Verse 4 says, "All the members do not have the same function," and the following verses tell us how to function. Even to show mercy and to extend hospitality to others is a function (vv. 8, 13). To do these things indicates that we are active members, not inactive ones. If we are active members who function all the time, the Body life will be very practical. If we do not function but merely meet together again and again, we will not have a real and practical church life. The genuine and practical church life depends on the function of the members. Romans 12 is a chapter on the Body, but it is the Body in function.

God's Will Being to Have the Body Life

Romans 12:1-2 tells us to present our bodies a living sacrifice and be transformed by the renewing of the mind "that you may prove what the will of God is, that which is good and well pleasing and perfect." This verse speaks of "the" will of God; the King James Version renders it as "that" will of God. God does not have many wills but only one will. What is the one will? In speaking of the will of God, many Christians wrongly apply this verse. Strictly speaking, this verse indicates that the will of God is to have the church life. If we mean business with the Lord, present ourselves bodily to Him, and are willing to be transformed in our soul—our mind, emotion, and will—we will realize what God's will is in this universe and on the earth. God's will is nothing less than to have the church, that is, to have a Body for His Son. When we see this, we will sacrifice everything for it, because we will realize that this is the unique will.

The more we read these verses, the more we can realize that this is what they mean. By reading the entire context of Romans 12 we can realize what "the" will, or "that" will, of God is. It is to have the Body life, the church. This is the will of God. Of course the will of God includes other things, but all the other matters are secondary. The primary item of God's will is the church. No matter how good we are or how many things we do, if we are not in the church, if we do not practice the church life and live for the church, we are not in the will of God. I say this with certainty; we will be outside of the will of God, even though we are doing something for God.

Although the things mentioned in chapters twelve through

sixteen may be considered the "wills" of God, the Body life is the foremost item. Chapters fourteen and fifteen tell us how to receive others, how to care for others, and how to avoid stumbling others, but all these matters are secondary. They depend on our practice of the church life. The first item that is revealed in chapters twelve through sixteen is the church, the Body, and all of the following items are supplementary to this will. Therefore, to prove what the will of God is, is to practice the church life. If we are proper members of the Body, acting and functioning in the church life, then we will have everything else. We will be persons in the will of God.

CHAPTER TWELVE

THE MAIN PRINCIPLES IN 1 CORINTHIANS

Scripture Reading: 1 Cor. 1:2, 9, 18, 22-24, 30; 2:2, 14-15; 3:1, 3

As we saw in the previous chapters, the first five books of the New Testament are a history of the universal man, Christ with the church. After this history, Romans gives us a full sketch of the definition of this universal man.

Following this sketch, 1 Corinthians presents cases and illustrations to show us that in this universal man there are two matters which are basically and vitally important: Christ and Christ crucified, or we may say, Christ and the cross. In 1:22-23a Paul says, "For indeed Jews require signs and Greeks seek wisdom, but we preach Christ crucified." *Christ crucified* refers not only to Christ Himself but Christ with His cross. In this universal man there is Christ on the positive side and the cross on the negative side. Without Christ and His cross it is impossible for the believers to realize the practical life of this universal man. The practical life of the universal man depends on the practical realization of Christ as everything to us on the positive side, and the cross as our all-inclusive termination on the negative side. Following Romans, therefore, 1 Corinthians gives us a lengthy illustration to show us how much we need to realize Christ as everything and to experience the cross of Christ in our daily walk, in our church service, and in everything.

THE CRUCIAL MATTERS
IN CHAPTERS ONE THROUGH THREE
Christ as Our Portion

There are a few key verses in the first three chapters of

this book. First Corinthians 1:2 says, "Our Lord Jesus Christ...who is theirs and ours." This short word is very meaningful, for it says that Christ is theirs and Christ is ours. To say that Christ is merely our Lord and their Lord is not the proper meaning of this verse. The right meaning is that Christ is our portion and their portion. This can be proved by verse 9, which says, "God is faithful, through whom you were called into the fellowship of His Son, Jesus Christ our Lord." To be called into the fellowship of Christ is to be called to share Christ, to partake of Christ. Christ has been given to us as our portion. The term *the allotted portion of the saints* is found in Colossians 1:12. The lot, the portion, of the saints is Christ Himself. The book of Colossians especially deals with this matter, telling us that the portion which we received from God is Christ Himself. No philosophy or any element of this world is our portion. Christ, not anything else, is our portion. Therefore, 1 Corinthians 1:9 says that we were called into the partaking of Christ as our portion. We have to partake of Him.

The Word of the Cross

Following this, verse 18 speaks of the word of the cross. This is the preaching of the cross. The ministry and preaching of the apostle Paul was a preaching of the cross. Paul preached not only Christ Himself but Christ with the cross.

Christ the Power and Wisdom of God

Verse 22 continues, "For indeed Jews require signs and Greeks seek wisdom." Signs are a matter of power; in order to perform signs, we need power. Wisdom in this verse indicates knowledge and the way to do things. If we have wisdom, we have the knowledge and also the way that enables us to do things. Power is one matter; the way to do something is another. With all things in this universe, there is the need of the power and the way. We may illustrate this with a car. We need gasoline within the car, and we also need to know how to drive the car.

Verse 24 says of Christ crucified, "But to those who are called, both Jews and Greeks, Christ the power of God and the wisdom of God." Christ is the power and energy of God, and He is also the wisdom and way of God. Christ is the power for us to do the things of God, and He is also the very wisdom, knowledge, and way for us to do them.

Christ Our Righteousness, Sanctification, and Redemption

Verse 30 continues, "But of Him you are in Christ Jesus, who became wisdom to us from God: both righteousness and sanctification and redemption." The King James Version renders the latter phrase as "wisdom, and righteousness, and sanctification, and redemption." However, the first *and* here is the Greek word *te,* which is better rendered as *both.* This construction indicates that wisdom is the heading, and under this heading there are three items—righteousness, sanctification, and redemption. Christ is God's wisdom to us, which includes righteousness for our past, sanctification for our present, and redemption for our future. Righteousness is for us to be justified at the time we believed. After being saved, Christ is our sanctification in our daily walk and in everything. The redemption mentioned here is the redemption of our body in the future (Rom. 8:23), because it is mentioned as the last of the three items. This redemption is Christ Himself.

Christ is our righteousness for the past. Christ is also our sanctification for the present; we are being sanctified in Christ. Then in the future, Christ will be our redemption; that is, our body will be redeemed in Christ. In this way we enjoy God's full salvation. These three matters are the items of Christ's being wisdom to us. This means that Christ is everything to us.

Jesus Christ, and This One Crucified

Chapter two goes on to say, "For I did not determine to know anything among you except Jesus Christ, and this One crucified" (v. 2). Paul indicated that he made the decision not to know anything but Christ and His cross.

The Fleshly Man, the Soulish Man, and the Spiritual Man

In 1:7 Paul says, "So that you do not lack in any gift, eagerly awaiting the revelation of our Lord Jesus Christ." The Corinthian believers were not lacking in any gift; they had all gifts. However, in chapter three Paul said, "And I, brothers, was not able to speak to you as to spiritual men, but as to fleshy, as to infants in Christ" (v. 1). Strictly speaking, the word used in this verse is not *fleshly* but *fleshy,* referring to one who lives entirely by the flesh. Verses 2-3 say, "I gave you milk to drink, not solid food, for you were not yet able to receive it. But neither yet now are you able, for you are still fleshly. For if there is jealousy and strife among you, are you not fleshly and do you not walk according to the manner of man?" Although the Corinthians had all the gifts, they were still infants in Christ, not only fleshly but fleshy.

In chapter two Paul says, "But a soulish man does not receive the things of the Spirit of God, for they are foolishness to him and he is not able to know them because they are discerned spiritually. But the spiritual man discerns all things, but he himself is discerned by no one" (vv. 14-15). In these two verses there are two kinds of persons: the soulish man and the spiritual man. Along with these two kinds of persons, there is the fleshly man in chapter three. These verses reveal the fleshly man, the soulish man, and the spiritual man.

THE MAIN PRINCIPLES OF 1 CORINTHIANS

The verses that we have mentioned are the key verses of the entire book of 1 Corinthians. On the positive side, they show us how we must realize Christ as everything in our daily walk and Christian service, and on the negative side, they show us that the cross is the only way to deal with all things other than Christ Himself. Second, they reveal that we may have the so-called gifts yet still be infants in Christ, not only childish but even fleshly in our Christian life. Third, they tell us that Christians can be three kinds of persons. We can and must be spiritual persons; we can be soulish persons but should not be; and we can be fleshly, even fleshy, persons, which is the worst. These are the three main points revealed to us in this book. The remainder of the book simply deals with a number of cases that illustrate these points.

Bible students agree that it is rather difficult to divide this book into proper sections. It is not divided into sections in the same way as Romans. As we have seen, two and a half chapters of Romans deal with condemnation. Then there are another two chapters that deal with justification. Following this are a few chapters concerning sanctification, and the last five chapters deal with the Body life. However, 1 Corinthians is not composed in this way. Rather, it is composed according to principles and main points. These principles are first that in the Christian life and service we must take Christ as everything, and all things other than Christ have to be dealt with by the cross in a practical way. Second, we should not pay attention to the gifts rather than Christ Himself. We may even have all the gifts yet still be babyish and fleshly. Third, we can be a spiritual man, a soulish man, or a fleshly man. Then this book gives us a number of cases to illustrate these three main points. Therefore, it is not necessary to divide this book into sections. We should simply keep in mind that it shows us three main points concerning the Christian life, which are proved by many cases.

EXPERIENCING CHRIST AS LIFE
AND EVERYTHING TO US

After the general sketch given to us in the book of Romans, the New Testament continues to show us by real cases that we as Christians must realize that Christ is everything to us in our daily life, church life, and church service. It is not a matter of gifts, doctrines, or anything other than Christ. Christ must be our power, and He must be our way. We are not called by God to share in signs, miracles, or gifts. Nor are we called by God to partake of wisdom, knowledge, doctrines, and teachings. Rather, we are called by God into the fellowship of Christ. The portion ordained and given to us by God is Christ Himself, not gifts, doctrine, knowledge, teaching, signs, miracles, or wisdom. Therefore, Paul at the very beginning of this book declares, "For indeed Jews require signs and Greeks seek wisdom, but we preach Christ crucified" (1:22-23a).

Many people think that they need power, wisdom, energy, and strength to do things. They feel that they need knowledge and the best way to do things. However, they may not know that Christ is the power, Christ is the wisdom, Christ is the energy, Christ is the strength, and Christ is the knowledge. Christ is also the way for us to do things. God has not given us anything other than Christ. Christ is the wisdom of God as righteousness for us to be justified in the past, as our sanctification in the present, and as our redemption in the future. Moreover, He is the power of God, the way, and everything. Paul even declared to the Corinthians that he determined not to give them anything but Christ and Christ crucified.

We all must be clear about this. If we look at today's Christianity, we can see that Christ as wisdom given to us by God has been very much neglected. Rather, the formal churches pay their attention to the proper forms in their practice. The fundamental churches pay their full attention to doctrines, teachings, and theology. Sometimes they even forget about Christ, yet they insist on their doctrine. Another category is the Pentecostal churches, which pay their attention to gifts, mainly one gift—speaking in tongues. Wherever we go, if we talk with people about Christ Himself, only the hungry, thirsty, and seeking ones appreciate what we say. Many others do not appreciate it and even condemn it as wrong teaching. However, we must realize that God's intention is not to give us forms, doctrines, or gifts. God's intention is to give Christ Himself as life and as everything to us. We must learn how to experience Christ. Have we ever been taught that Christ is righteousness, sanctification, and redemption to us? We need much time to realize, learn, and experience these three items.

Several hymns today teach wrongly by speaking of "the righteousness of Christ." However, there is not such a term found in the New Testament. It is not a matter of the righteousness of Christ, but Christ Himself being righteousness to us. What is the difference between the righteousness of Christ and Christ as righteousness? To receive merely the righteousness of Christ is too objective. In this case, Christ could have given us this righteousness and then departed to the heavens, leaving us only the Holy Spirit as His "representative." This is not the proper understanding. Righteousness is Christ Himself; we can never separate it from Christ. If we have Christ, we have righteousness; if we do not have Christ, we do not have righteousness.

Consider the parable in Luke 15:11-32. The robe in verse 22 signifies that Christ is our righteousness to cover us and to justify us, thus enabling us to match the Father's glory. However, this is not all. Christ is also the fattened calf for us to enjoy and partake of (v. 23). We put on Christ as the robe, and we take Christ in as the calf. It is not the righteousness of Christ that saves us; it is Christ Himself as righteousness that saves us.

We must learn that Christ Himself is everything to us. He Himself is righteousness, and He Himself is also sanctification. In order to realize the real meaning of sanctification, we must know Christ, and we must know how to serve Christ, how to enjoy Christ, how to apply Christ, and how to experience Christ. If we do not know how to apply and experience Christ, we simply do not know the practical meaning of sanctification. The practical meaning of sanctification is Christ Himself experienced by us. The Christ whom we experience day by day is the way, the sanctification, and the redemption.

Nearly all of the Christian hymns written about the second coming of Christ are too objective. They simply speak of this event as being glorious because the glorious One will come back. Rarely can we find one hymn that tells us something about the Lord's second coming in the subjective way of life. The glory of the Lord's second coming is actually Christ Himself. Christ in us is the hope of glory (Col. 1:27). Christ Himself is the glory, and this glory today is in us. He Himself is the glory, and He Himself is the hope. He is the redemption of our body.

All the forms, if they are necessary, and all the doctrines and gifts are for Christ. What God intends to work into us and to have us experience is nothing other than Christ. We have to learn how to appropriate Christ in our daily walk and in all our service.

APPLYING THE CROSS OF CHRIST

We must also experience the cross. The enjoyment of Christ is something on the positive side, while the cross is on the negative side to deal with all the things that are not Christ Himself. The old creation, the self, the flesh, the natural man, and the soulish life all need to be dealt with by the cross. If we want to take Christ every day, we need to experience the cross. Christ and His cross are the unique solution to all the problems in the Christian life and church life. All problems in the Christian life and in the church can be solved only by Christ with His cross.

If a married couple is not able to get along well, this indicates that they are short of the experience of Christ and the cross. To be sure, if they learn how to experience Christ by taking the cross, they will live harmoniously. The primary problem in the church, in the work, among the co-workers, and among the brothers and sisters is due to one thing—the lack of experiencing Christ by taking the cross. It is the same in a family. If all the members of a family appropriate Christ in their daily life and take the cross, everything will be right among them. If the co-workers and responsible brothers in a church realize how to take Christ as everything and experience the cross, everything will also be right with them.

Teachings cannot solve our problems. The more we give people teachings, the more problems and troubles we create. For example, if we come to a husband to teach him to love his wife, he may say, "You had better tell my wife to submit to me." If we then go to his wife to teach her to submit to her husband, she may say, "You must tell my husband that he needs to love his wife." All of this is mere doctrine. I saw all of these things, and in the early days of my service I failed many times in this way. When I talked with a sister, I would tell her to read Ephesians 5, which says that she must submit to her husband. Then she would charge me, saying, "Don't teach the sisters only. Go teach my husband." Then I would go to the husband and teach him also, and he would tell me to go teach his wife. Sometimes teachings help in a small way, but they do not solve our problems thoroughly. The only answer to all of our problems is Christ and the cross.

Many times I have tried to help people in another, better way. I would speak to a sister, saying, "Sister, do you love the Lord? Do you know where He is? He is within you. Would you like to contact the Lord, have some fellowship with Him, and offer yourself to Him?" We should forget about a sister's quarrel with her husband and simply help her to take Christ and to realize that her old man, her flesh, and her soulish life all must be put on the cross. Then we may check to see if she knows how to realize the cross in her daily life. Although this is a teaching, it is a different kind of teaching. It is a teaching that helps her to realize Christ and apply the cross. In this way the problems will be solved, not by teaching but by Christ and the cross.

All the problems with Christians and all the problems in the churches can be solved only by Christ experienced and the cross applied. There were divisions among the Corinthians because those believers paid their attention to gifts, signs, knowledge, and wisdom, but they very much neglected Christ and the cross. Therefore, there were many problems. The more gifts and knowledge we have, the more problems we have. All the divisions and denominations were produced out of gifted persons. In the past four or five hundred years, whenever there was a deeper, gifted person, a division or sect was often created, and the more gifted the person was, the greater the division was.

All the gifts mentioned in 1 Corinthians are spiritual gifts, not natural gifts. We may think that spiritual gifts can do no harm. In actuality, the gifts themselves do no harm, but the persons who are gifted often do a great deal of harm by the gifts. From the time of the Reformation through the present day, there has rarely been a very gifted person who has not created a denomination, sect, or division. We cannot say absolutely that there has not been an exception, but it is rather difficult for us to point one out. Almost every famous gifted person in the past centuries created a division by his gifts.

Although we do need the gifts, we should not pay attention to the gifts. We must pay our full attention to Christ Himself. All the gifts are for Christ. The Corinthians were not lacking in any gift. Chapters twelve and fourteen especially show us how many gifts were exercised and practiced among them. However, chapter three says that they were fleshly and babyish. In these days we must be aware that we should not pay attention to the gifts. If we pay attention to the gifts, divisions will come. Although the gifts themselves are good, it depends on how we handle them. We must realize that Christ is the center, and all the gifts are for Christ.

BEING A SPIRITUAL MAN

The third main principle in 1 Corinthians is that a believer can be spiritual, soulish, or fleshly, even fleshy. Simply speaking, a spiritual person is one who lives and walks by his spirit, whose soul is always subdued by the spirit, and whose body, the flesh, is always under the control of the strong will of his renewed soul. Such a one lives, walks, and acts by the spirit with his soul subdued and with the flesh controlled.

A soulish person, on the other hand, is neither fleshly nor spiritual but simply natural. This kind of person is one who lives by the soul, that is, by the intellect, by the mind, by the reasonings, by the will, and by the emotion. Whereas there is nothing sinful or fleshly with him, there is neither anything spiritual. He is neutral to being fleshly, and he is neutral to being spiritual. He does things, lives, and acts always by his intellect, by his will, or by his emotion.

Such a person cannot understand the things of God (2:14). There is no potential for him to know the spiritual things because he does not have the spiritual discernment. He simply cannot discern spiritual things because he does not exercise his spirit, which is the spiritual organ to know the spiritual things. For a soulish man to discern spiritual things may be compared to exercising our ears to substantiate color. It is impossible to listen to colors; this is to exercise the wrong organ. There is no potential for our ears to realize colors. If we want to substantiate color, we need to exercise our eyes. In the same way, we cannot know spiritual things if we live by the soul, by our mentality, reasoning, intellect, mind, will, or emotion. No matter how good we may be, we are still not spiritual; we are soulish.

A fleshly person is one fully controlled by the flesh. His soul is controlled by his flesh, and his spirit is covered by his soul. This person acts, lives, and does things by the flesh. The Corinthian believers were not only fleshly but even fleshy. There is a difference between being fleshly and fleshy. The case mentioned in chapters one and three, for example, involves fleshly believers. These persons caused divisions and strife, saying, "I am of Paul, and I of Apollos, and I of Cephas, and I of Christ" (1:12). Those persons with jealousy and strife were fleshly (3:3). The cases in chapters five and six, however, are more serious, involving people who were not only fleshly but fleshy, those who lived, walked, and did things by the fallen flesh. *Fleshy* denotes a person who does evil things directly from his flesh. *Fleshly* denotes a person who does things under the influence of the nature of the flesh and partakes of the character of the flesh. Quarreling, making divisions, and envying are matters done under the influence of the flesh. However, to do the evil things by the fallen flesh, as recorded in chapter five, is to be fleshy, even like an animal.

All of this indicates that we can do things either by the spirit as a spiritual man, by the soul as soulish persons, by the flesh directly as fleshy persons, or under the influence of the flesh as fleshly persons. This is why Paul used these four different words in chapters two and three: *soulish* (2:14), *spiritual* (v. 15), *fleshy* (3:1), and *fleshly* (v. 3).

I hope that you will keep these principles in mind and put them into practice. In the next chapter we will see at least ten problems in 1 Corinthians that illustrate how much we need to take Christ on the positive side and experience the cross on the negative side. All the time we must look to the Lord's help to realize that as Christians we must always learn to apply Christ as everything in our family, in the church, in our daily walk, and in the church service. In addition, before we quarrel with others, do something for others, or deal with others, we must learn to apply the cross to ourselves. Moreover, we must realize that although we may have the best things, such as gifts, signs, knowledge, and wisdom, those things are not Christ Himself. It is not a matter of these things; we must have Christ. If we do not have Christ, we are finished; we may still remain infants in Christ and fleshly. In addition, we must realize that even though we are the children of God, we may still be something other than spiritual; we may be soulish, fleshly, and even fleshy. We must be burdened and trust the Lord that we may all walk in the spirit.

CHAPTER THIRTEEN

THE PRINCIPLES AND CASES IN 1 CORINTHIANS

Scripture Reading: 1 Cor. 1:2, 9, 23-24, 30, 7; 3:1-3; 2:14-15; 1:12-13; 5:1; 6:7; 7:32; 9:1, 4-5; 10:17, 23; 11:3, 29; 12:12-13; 15:3-4, 54; 16:1-2; 5:7; 10:3-4; 9:24; 3:12, 15, 9

First Corinthians is composed of basic principles and a number of cases. In order to know its real content and insight, we must first grasp its principles and then see its cases, which illustrate the principles in many ways. There are eleven cases in this book, and in addition to the main principles and cases, there are several secondary principles.

CHRIST AND HIS CROSS

As we examine the cases in this book, we must keep the main principles in mind. As we saw in the previous chapter, the first principle is Christ on the positive side and the cross to deal with the negative things. In the church life these two matters are very basic. If we do not have a vision from God that Christ is everything, it is very difficult to understand what the real meaning of the Christian walk and church life are. Christ Himself is the reality, center, and central vision of our Christian walk and church life. He is the portion to us from God.

God does not intend to give us anything other than Christ. If God has given us other things, those things are not for themselves; they are for us to realize Christ. All things, such as forms, knowledge, gifts, and functions, are to help us realize Christ, know Christ, partake of Christ, apply Christ, and experience Christ. God's intention is to give us Christ as our full portion. Christ is both theirs and ours (1:2), and we have been called into the fellowship, that is, the participation, of Christ (v. 9). Moreover, God has made Christ wisdom to us, including righteousness for our past, sanctification for the present, and redemption for the future (v. 30). In God's salvation, purpose, and plan Christ is everything to us as power and wisdom (v. 24). Now we must learn to know Him in such a way. In our daily walk and in the church life, we must learn how to apply Christ as everything and to experience Him. This is on the positive side.

On the other side, there are many negative matters. Sin, self, the natural life, the old man, the worldly things, Satan, and darkness all must be dealt with by the cross. Christ is not Christ only; He is "Christ crucified" (v. 23), that is, Christ with the cross. To experience Christ today, there must be the application of His cross. His cross is the only way to prepare the ground for Him to be everything to us. In order to experience Him, apply Him, and take Him as everything, we must experience the cross of Christ to deal with all the negative things.

The first main principle in this book is Christ and the cross. After Paul gives us a general sketch of the Christian life in Romans, he gives us the book of 1 Corinthians to show us the main principles for the life and walk of the universal man—Christ with His Body. This Body of this universal man must realize how to take Christ as everything on the positive side and how to experience the cross daily on the negative side.

HAVING KNOWLEDGE AND GIFTS BUT BEING INFANTS IN CHRIST

The second principle in this book is that no matter how many gifts and how much knowledge we may have received, we are still infants and fleshly if we do not know how to experience Christ with His cross (v. 7; 3:1-3). This is a serious matter, which is made very clear in this book. This is also contrary to the concepts in Christianity today. Many in Christianity insist that what we need are gifts, knowledge, doctrines, and teaching. However, in this book the apostle Paul tells us clearly that regardless of how much knowledge and how many gifts we have, even if we do not lack in any gift and have all knowledge, we are fleshly and infants in Christ if we do not realize how to experience Christ and His cross. This principle must be impressed into us.

In recent years I have been fighting the battle for this principle. I have met many people who have doctrines and teachings in their mentality, and I have met many so-called gifted persons. I also have seen many strange things and many healings. By these I realize that what the apostle Paul wrote in 1 Corinthians is one hundred percent true. People may have much knowledge and many gifts yet still not know how to experience Christ in their daily walk, apply Christ in their church life, and apply the cross in their daily affairs. Regrettably, such persons are still childish, shallow, and on many occasions fleshly.

Although knowledge and gifts help to some extent, the church life and our daily walk are not a matter of knowledge or gifts but a matter of the real and practical experience of Christ under the working of the cross. We all must learn this and pay our full attention to this. If we experience Christ under the working of the cross in such a way, we will be progressively equipped with the proper and adequate knowledge, and whatever kind of gifts we need will be measured to us by God. There is no need for us to covet knowledge and the gifts; we must simply experience Christ under the work of the cross. God, the sovereign One, knows how much knowledge we need and what kind of gifts we need. He will measure a certain amount of knowledge and certain gifts to us to meet the need. This is the proper way to have knowledge and gifts.

In the New Testament there is the record of at least one church that stressed knowledge and gifts more than the real experience of Christ and the cross. They were too much ahead in knowledge and in the gifts. This is why the second main principle is set forth in this book.

FOUR KINDS OF CHRISTIANS

Third, a regenerated person can be one of four kinds of Christians. He can be a spiritual man, a soulish or natural man, a fleshly man, or a fleshy man who is like an animal with no shame or feeling. This book gives us many illustrations to show us what a spiritual, soulish, fleshly, or fleshy man is. First Corinthians records all four kinds of people. By his writings, the apostle Paul is spontaneously manifested as a spiritual man. He did not boast in himself, but in order to know the history of this apostle, we must read 1 and 2 Corinthians. These two books may be considered Paul's autobiography, depicting what kind of person he is. His motive, his intention, his character, his real being, his activities, and his heavenly and spiritual ambition are all portrayed here. Therefore, at least one person in this book, the apostle Paul, is a spiritual person. In this book there are also soulish people, exercising their mentality, reasonings, and knowledge to try to realize the spiritual things. In addition, there are also many fleshly believers in this book, and there are at least a few who are fleshy, as illustrated in chapters five and six.

We must keep the above three main principles in mind when we come to the cases in this book. Then we will understand this book easily and in the proper way.

THE CASES IN 1 CORINTHIANS

The Problem of Divisions

With these three main principles in view, we can now consider each of the cases. The first case is the problem of division and sects (1:10—4:21). Some in Corinth said that they were of Paul, others were of Apollos, others were of Cephas, and others even claimed that they were of Christ (1:12). These were divisions or sects which arose from the flesh, because their flesh had not been dealt with. Their flesh lacked the real working of the cross. To say, "I am of Paul" proves that a person is fleshly, that there is no mark of the cross on this person. If the cross is applied to our flesh, we will never say that we are of Paul or of anyone else.

On the negative side, the flesh has to be dealt with, while on the positive side, we must know that Christ is not divided. Verse 13 asks, "Is Christ divided?" If we know Christ, apply Christ, and experience Christ, we will realize that He is one. Not only so, but because the Head is one, the Body is also one.

Christ is one, and the church is one. To be sure, if we know Christ, we will know the oneness of the Body. Why are there many divisions today? It is simply due to the fact that people do not know Christ on the positive side and do not experience the cross on the negative side. If we know Christ and apply the cross to our flesh, there will be no divisions. Spontaneously we will realize the reality of the oneness of the Body of Christ. Therefore, the principle that governs the first case is Christ and the cross.

The Problem of a Fleshy Brother

The second case is that of a person who was not only fleshly but fleshy (5:1-13). According to the record of chapters five and six, the fleshy cases were of several shameful kinds. Although they are mentioned in the Word of God, they are not pleasant to read. No doubt, people can be so fleshy because they neglect the experience of Christ, and they forfeit the experience of applying the cross to their flesh. We cannot be fleshy if we are truly under the work of the cross and experiencing Christ.

The Problem of Lawsuits among Believers

The next case recorded in this book concerns a lawsuit, in which brothers took one another to the law (6:1-11). It is a shame for brothers to go to court to sue one another. Verse 7 says, "Already then it is altogether a defeat to you that you have lawsuits with one another. Why not rather be wronged? Why not rather be defrauded?" This is the teaching of the cross. Even if a brother defrauds us, we should be willing to suffer loss and take the experience of the cross. We should not lose the experience of the cross by filing a lawsuit. We may win the case and gain some material things, but we will lose the precious experience of the cross. We should choose to suffer and experience the cross rather than to gain from a lawsuit. This is the practical experience of the cross.

We may talk about the cross, but one day a brother may defraud us. Should we go to court and sue him? This is not the proper way. The proper way is to suffer the loss by being defrauded. Although we may suffer the loss of material things, we experience the cross and gain Christ. This is more precious, and in this way we give glory to God. However, if we go to court, that is a real shame to the Lord's name. Those Corinthian brothers went to the law because they neglected the experience of Christ and His cross. If they had applied the first principle, the principle of Christ and the cross, there would have been no lawsuit.

The Problem of the Abuse of Freedom

The fourth case dealt with by this Epistle is the abuse of freedom of foods and in the body (vv. 12-20). In dealing with this problem, Paul tells the Corinthians that our bodies are members of Christ (v. 15), we are one spirit with the Lord (v. 17), and our body is a temple of the Holy Spirit (v. 19).

The Problem of Marriage Life

The fifth case in this book deals with marriage life (7:1-40). In the entire sixty-six books of the Bible there is no other chapter which deals with marriage as clearly and inclusively as this chapter. If we read this portion carefully, we will see that the same basic principle applies to marriage. Without Christ and His cross no problems with marriage can ever be settled. Even if we could settle a problem, it would not be in a proper way. Similarly, whether one marries or does not marry can only be settled by experiencing Christ and the cross. We must apply the cross to ourselves and take Christ as our life even in the matter of marriage. Then we will be clear how to solve the problems.

This is why we emphasize that in reading these chapters, we must realize and apply the principle behind them. Then we can be clear about what they mean. For example, verse 32 says, "The unmarried cares for the things of the Lord, how he may please the Lord." This is an experience of Christ and the cross. If we experience Christ and the cross, we will know how to please the Lord in the matter of marriage. Whether or not we marry, whom we marry, and how to maintain our marriage life all depend on how we please the Lord by experiencing Christ and His cross.

The Problem of Eating

The sixth case is concerned with the matter of eating (8:1—11:1). The case of division is fleshly, and the cases in chapters five and six are fleshy. The case in chapters eight through ten, however, is both fleshy and fleshly. This kind of eating has much to do with the flesh. There were two kinds of believers who had no consideration for others in the matter of eating. Certain believers were addicted to their way of eating, so no doubt they were fleshy. Others, however, were not fleshy but strong in their conscience. They did not care what foods they ate, but neither did they care for the conscience of the weaker ones. They acted independently and thus became fleshly. If we read these chapters carefully, we will see that they deal more with the fleshly aspect of eating.

Some in Corinth were debating about the matter of eating not because they were addicted to a certain way of eating but because of the problem of the conscience. Some believers who were not strong in their conscience felt that food sacrificed to idols had something to do with idol worship and that if they ate it, they would share in the idols. Although this is a good thought, it is according to a weak conscience. Others were strong concerning eating, but they were careless about others' feelings. It is as if they said, "Idols mean nothing. All things were created by God for us. Even if the food is sacrificed to the idols, it is still good for us to eat." Toward themselves they were right, but toward others they were careless because they were fleshly. They insisted on eating without caring for others' weak conscience, so they stumbled the weaker ones. Although they had the right to eat, they should have taken care of others.

Therefore, chapter nine follows chapter eight to present the apostle Paul as an example. Although he had the right to do many lawful things, yet for others' sake, he would not use those rights (vv. 1, 4-5). This is an example to those believers who, though they are strong in their conscience and have the right to eat things offered to idols, need to take care of others.

In the case of eating sacrifices to idols, the first principle of this book is again needed. We need to experience Christ and His cross. To experience the cross is to deal not only with wrong and negative things but also with lawful things, right things, and even our own rights. It was right for certain ones to eat food offered to the idols, and they had the right to do it. Idols mean nothing, and all of those foods were created by God as something good to eat. Moreover, in denying the significance of the idols they seemed to be eating for the glory of God. Nevertheless, we must learn how to experience the cross even in dealing with lawful things so that we may take care of others.

This is a deeper experience of the cross. We may have the thought that the experience of the cross is mainly to deal with wrong things, wrong attitudes, and other wrong matters. However, this case is an illustration showing us that although we have the full legal right to do certain things, we need to take the dealing of the cross for others' sake.

In this case, as well as in the others, the apostle Paul cared for the building up of the Body (10:17, 23). Although we have the right to do many lawful things, we need to take care of the building up of the Body and the members of the Body. We should not do anything to damage the building up of the Body or the relationships between the members. In this light, the meaning of this case is very transparent.

The Problem of Head Covering

The seventh case found in 1 Corinthians involves the matter of head covering (11:2-16). The problem of head covering is a debate not only of today; it was there already in the first century.

Head covering is related to the headship, the lordship, of Christ in the universe. Verse 3 says, "But I want you to know that Christ is the head of every man, and the man is the head of the woman, and God is the head of Christ." Therefore, there is the need of the woman to have her head covered. Here again we must apply the first principle of this book. The only ones who are willing to cover their head are those who know how to experience the cross to deal with their self and how to take Christ as everything to be their Head. Covering the head is a matter of experiencing Christ as the Head. This includes taking Christ as life and everything and experiencing the cross.

The best way to help people realize the real meaning of head covering is to help them to experience Christ as life, as the Head, and as everything. It is also to help them to realize the real experience of the cross in order to deal with the natural man and the self. If we are able to help the saints in these two matters, the sisters will be not only willing but also obliged to cover their heads, especially when they pray. However, we must give people the full liberty. On the one hand, we should not be "Pharisees" or make others to be "Pharisees," while on the other hand, we should not lower the standard.

The Problem of the Lord's Supper

The next case in 1 Corinthians concerns the Lord's supper (11:17-34). The case of head covering concerns the Head (v. 3), while the Lord's supper (the Lord's table) concerns the Body. In this way, chapter eleven deals with the universal man—the Head and the Body. In principle, we all have to be right with the Head, and we also must be right with the Body. If we are wrong with the Lord's supper, we are wrong with the Body because we do not discern the body (v. 29).

The loaf on the table has two meanings. The Lord's supper is for the remembrance of the Lord Himself. Therefore, at the Lord's supper the loaf signifies the Lord's physical body crucified on the cross for our redemption. We view the loaf in remembrance of the Lord Himself. The Lord's table, however, is for the communion, the fellowship, of the saints; it is the Lord's feast for the fellowship of the Body. Verse 16 of chapter ten says, "The bread which we break, is it not the fellowship of the body of Christ?", and verse 17 says, "We who are many are one Body." While we fellowship with one another around the Lord's table, we view the loaf as the symbol of the universal, mystical Body of Christ, which is the church (Eph. 4:4). Thus, one aspect of the loaf is for the remembrance of the Lord Himself, while the other aspect is for fellowship with all the saints in the one mystical Body.

Therefore, to discern the body in 1 Corinthians 11:29 has two meanings. Whenever we come to partake of the loaf, we must discern that it is not something ordinary, because it symbolizes the Lord's body crucified for us on the cross. We should not partake of it as we would an ordinary piece of bread in the morning. Rather, we should partake of it with reverence. Moreover, we must also discern the universal, mystical Body of Christ. This is why we should not partake of the "communion" in the denominations, because they are divisions. To partake of their "communion" is to partake of their division. That is not the Lord's table but a table of division. The Lord's table must be on the proper ground, representing not a sect or denomination but the Body.

Although there may be a "communion" in a denominational church with thousands of members who are all genuinely saved, that table still does not represent the one Body. Rather, it represents the Lutheran, Presbyterian, or Baptist denomination. Regardless of how large their membership is, it still represents that denomination. On the contrary, if there are only three or four brothers standing on the ground of oneness, representing the Body, what they have is the proper Lord's table in the discernment of the Body. This is the proper meaning of *discern the body* in 11:29.

We must have a proper relationship with the Head and the Body. The matter of head covering ensures that we have a right relationship with the Head, and the Lord's table keeps us in a right relationship with the Lord's Body. Today many Christians pay attention to the remembrance of the Lord, but they neglect and even oppose the matter of the Body. Therefore, their table does not represent the Body; it represents their denomination. This nullifies this whole portion of 1 Corinthians; the headship is gone, and the Body is gone. This is the subtle will of the devil, the enemy of God. May the Lord be merciful to us. We must be humble to submit ourselves to His headship and be submissive to the Body; that is, we must be right with the Head and with the Body. We can do this only by experiencing Christ and taking the cross.

The Problem of the Gifts

The ninth case Paul dealt with in 1 Corinthians is the exercise of the gifts (12:1—14:40). Even the spiritual gifts can be a problem to the Body of Christ. It all depends on how we exercise these gifts.

First, we need to realize that all the spiritual gifts and the exercise of the gifts must be for the Body. First Corinthians 12:12 says, "For even as the body is one and has many members, yet all the members of the body, being many, are one body, so also is the Christ." All the gifts with their functions and exercise must be for the Body. Moreover, we should realize that not only is the Head Christ but the Body also is Christ. Following this, verse 13 says, "For also in one Spirit we were all baptized into one Body, whether Jews or Greeks, whether slaves or free." This tells us that all the gifts from the Holy Spirit are for the Body. Regrettably, however, the gifts today often distract believers from the Body rather than build up the Body. What should be used for building becomes a distraction; this is wrong. The more we have the gifts, function with the gifts, and exercise the gifts, the more we need to build up the Body. All the believers must be focused on the Body. We should not distract any member from the Body by using our gift.

The best way for us to exercise the gifts is in the way of love (13:1-13). Love is the best, excellent way. Real love is Christ with the cross. In order to exercise the genuine love toward others, we must experience Christ with the cross. Our self has to be dealt with, and we must take Christ as everything. Then we will know how to love others. Even with the exercise of the gifts, we may not have love. On the contrary, instead of loving others, we may simply speak in tongues every day with no concern for others. If we read chapters twelve through fourteen carefully, we will see that the intention of the writer is that we would prefer to have love rather than to exercise the gifts. If our exercise of spiritual gifts does not build up others or profit others, we should be willing to drop the gifts and exercise our love toward others. This is the best way for us to exercise our gifts, because their purpose is to build up the Body. If our exercise of the gifts does not fulfill this purpose, we should be willing to drop them. If love builds up others more than gifts do, we should exercise love rather than the gifts.

Here again we must apply the first principle of this book. The person who has the gifts must be dealt with. Then he will have the best way to exercise the gifts, which is love. This love, no doubt, is Christ with the experience of the cross.

The Problem concerning Resurrection

The tenth case involves the matter of resurrection (15:1-58). It is surprising that even a real Christian would not believe that there is a resurrection. These were not "modernists"; the Corinthians were genuine Christians, but among them there were some who did not believe in the fact of resurrection. This case is related to the third principle in this book, the principle of being spiritual, soulish, or fleshly. These few were soulish persons because they tried to reason concerning the resurrection by their mental understanding. We cannot understand spiritual things with our mentality, our soulish mind; if we try to, we are soulish.

In this chapter there is a spiritual and heavenly revelation that not only confirms the resurrection but reveals the ultimate consummation of the Body of Christ. The ultimate consummation of the Body of Christ will transpire on the day Christ returns and life swallows up death (v. 54). Here, therefore, it is not only a matter of resurrection, but a matter of life swallowing up death. At that time the Body of Christ will be in its full consummation, testifying what Christ is and how much He is.

The Problem of Material Possessions

The last case dealt with by Paul in 1 Corinthians is the case of giving and receiving material possessions (16:1-9). The matter of giving and receiving material things is very practical. Our Christian life and church service must be filled with giving and receiving. We should not store up for ourselves all the things we receive from God. Rather, we must give to others, passing on what we have and caring for others. If we are not this kind of believer, we are wrong. If with regard to material possessions we are defeated, we are not spiritual believers but fleshly or soulish. If the Lord would give us a certain amount of money, we should give to others to take care of the Body. Even giving and receiving is a matter of the Body life.

In dealing with material possessions, we must learn to pray, seek the Lord's guidance, and take care of the situation in the Body and of the saints' needs. We must be concerned for the Lord's children and His Body to the extent that if we receive a certain amount of money, we would give some to others and then spend the rest, not for ourselves but for the Body.

According to verse 2, we should offer our gifts on the first day of the week. This is the eighth day, which signifies resurrection. That we make our offering on the day of resurrection indicates that our giving should be done in resurrection. We should not offer in an old way but in a new way. We should not offer in the principle of the seventh day, which represents the old creation, but in the principle of the first day, which symbolizes the newness of resurrection. Even if we give something on the Lord's Day, in the sight of God it still may not be in the principle of the Lord's Day. It may be something of the first day of the old week, in waste, emptiness, and darkness (Gen. 1:2). There may be no life or light in that giving. This is to add "honey" to our offerings, which is the sweetness of the flesh and of our old nature in our friendliness with others. This is wrong. We must offer whatever the Lord gives as a surplus in material things in the way of resurrection. The flesh and the old creation must be thoroughly dealt with.

Sometimes we may pass on good things to our intimate relatives in order to meet a particular need. Although this may be according to the guidance of the Lord, there may be no imparting of life. Rather, we should be willing to give our surplus to the co-workers, to the Lord's servants, and to the Lord's people with whom we have no relationship in the flesh, but with whom there is a real relationship in the Body. We give to others not because we love them in a natural way or out of a friendship or relationship, but because of the Lord's burden, interest, and work. We give not in the old creation but in the new creation, not on the seventh day but on the eighth day. In principle, we give on the Lord's Day.

Here again, even in the matter of giving and receiving, our self must be dealt with by the cross. We must give all the ground to Christ and give all the praise to Him as our Head. Then our giving will be done in the proper way. Of course, literally speaking, the Christians in the ancient time came together on the Lord's Day to meet. This is the literal meaning of the Lord's Day, but there is a spiritual meaning as well, which is that we do nothing in the way of old religion.

In the foregoing eleven cases, there are spiritual persons, soulish persons, fleshly persons, and fleshy persons. We can apply these four conditions to all the persons in this book.

SOME SECONDARY PRINCIPLES

A Picture of the Real Condition of the Believers

There are also some principles in 1 Corinthians which are important but secondary, comparatively speaking. First, this book gives us a picture of the real condition of the believers. It is very similar to that of the people of Israel in the Old Testament. According to the history of the Jews, they were saved by the Passover in Egypt, delivered out of Egypt, and brought into the wilderness. After wandering in the wilderness, they were commanded to press on into the good land of Canaan. The history of the people of Israel is repeated in 1 Corinthians. In chapter five the Corinthians enjoyed Christ as their Passover (v. 7). Now we, like they, are enjoying the Feast of Unleavened Bread, so we must purge out the old leaven.

Chapter ten again records that the Corinthians were the same as the people of Israel. They enjoyed the Passover, were delivered from Egypt, and were brought into the wilderness. However, almost all of them were fleshly and soulish. Very few were spiritual. The accounts in the Old and New Testaments exactly correspond to one another. Just as God told the people of Israel to press on into the good land, the apostle Paul told the Corinthians to run the race and pursue the goal. We need to read the last part of chapter nine together with the first part of chapter ten; these two portions should not be separated. The end of chapter nine tells us that there is a race to run (vv. 24-27), and chapter ten tells us that the Israelites ran their race and failed (vv. 1-13). Therefore, today we must run the race in a better way. The better way is to forget about the flesh, deny the natural, soulish life, and press on into the spirit. Then we will reach the goal, Christ.

Being Rewarded in Addition to Being Saved

In this book there is the principle that we take Christ as our Passover, our Redeemer, to be saved from God's condemnation and from worldly occupation. To be saved from Egypt is one thing, but to press on to enter into God's fullness, to enjoy Christ, to attain to the goal, and to receive the reward are another thing. To receive a reward at the end of the race is an additional matter. Although we may be redeemed, at the end of the race we may suffer loss.

First Corinthians 3:14-15 says, "If anyone's work which he has built upon the foundation remains, he will receive a reward; if anyone's work is consumed, he will suffer loss, but he himself will be saved, yet so as through fire." Here it is a matter of receiving not salvation but the reward. If our work does not remain, it will be burned. This work is in the nature of wood, grass, and stubble (v. 12). Fleshly and worldly work will be burned, and we ourselves may suffer loss. When we speak this word, some may accuse us of teaching purgatory. However, regardless of how hard this word sounds, we must receive it. We do not care about people's accusations. We simply want to present the Lord's word to His people. We must not be deceived by our human thought. This portion of the word clearly tells us that we can be genuinely saved yet suffer loss through fire. What *fire* means, only the Lord knows, but there is such a thing.

Here is the principle that to be saved is one thing, but to be rewarded or suffer loss through fire even though we are saved is another. The children of Israel were saved by the Passover lamb and delivered out of Egypt, and they enjoyed the manna and the living water from the riven rock. Chapter ten tells us that today we too enjoy Christ as manna and the riven rock from whom the living water flows for our enjoyment day by day (vv. 3-4, 11). However, we may be exactly like the Israelites and come short of God's intention. In this case, we may not receive the reward of the fullness of the riches of the good land but may suffer a certain kind of loss.

This is what the Lord's word presents in a very pure way. Although we are definitely saved, we must be aware that there is a race before us that we all have to run. Even the apostle Paul himself said that he had to be careful how he ran the race (9:24-27). He was concerned that while others would be helped by his teaching, he himself would lose the race. Salvation is one thing, but to run the race and receive the reward or suffer loss is absolutely another.

Being God's Cultivated Land, God's Building

Another principle found in this book is in chapter three. Verse 9 says that we are God's cultivated land and God's building. As God's "crop" we need to grow. We have Christ as the seed of life sown into us. We also have the Holy Spirit as the living water to water us. Now we need to grow as God's farm and be built up as God's building.

CHAPTER FOURTEEN

THE MINISTRY AND THE MINISTERS
IN 2 CORINTHIANS

Scripture Reading: 2 Cor. 3:3, 6, 17-18; 4:7, 10-11, 16; 6:4-10; 11:23-29; 12:7-10; 13:14

A LIVING MINISTRY
TO WRITE LIVING LETTERS OF CHRIST

Second Corinthians 3:3 says, "Since you are being manifested that you are a letter of Christ ministered by us, inscribed not with ink but with the Spirit of the living God; not in tablets of stone but in tablets of hearts of flesh." This word indicates that something of Christ has been wrought into people to make them living letters of Christ. This is the work of a living ministry, not that of any kind of gift. I have never seen a person who had the life of Christ wrought into him merely by a gift. We cannot minister Christ into others merely by gift, teaching, word, or knowledge. Rather, it must be by something of Christ that has been wrought into us to make us not only the ministers of Christ but also the ministry of Christ. We, the persons, become the living ministry of Christ. When we minister, we not only pass on the knowledge about Christ to others, but we minister Christ Himself through the word into them.

This kind of ministry is one which works Christ into people so that they become the living letters of Christ. They are composed as letters not merely by knowledge or word but of the very essence, the very element of Christ. Something of Christ Himself as the Spirit has been wrought into the life and nature of His people so that they become the living letters of Christ. These letters are not inscribed with ink, that is, not with the letter of knowledge. They are written with the Spirit of the living God, with God Himself as life. In order to minister in this way, merely to have knowledge is not good enough. We must be in the spirit. Then when we speak, preach, and teach, the element, the essence, of the Spirit is ministered into people and wrought into people so that they become the living letters of Christ.

MINISTERS NOT OF THE LETTER
BUT OF THE SPIRIT AND LIFE

Verse 6 says, "Who has also made us sufficient as ministers of a new covenant, ministers not of the letter but of the Spirit; for the letter kills, but the Spirit gives life." There is an important principle here. We should not deal with the letter of the law. We should not pay attention to the mere letter, because the letter kills. It is the Spirit that gives life.

The Letter Killing
by Being Something Other Than Life

We may not fully understand the deeper meaning of *kills* in this verse. If we pay attention to things other than the life of God, that is a real killing. To kill is to put life into a position of not working, to cause life to be out of function. We may feel that to bring in death is a killing, but even if we do not bring in death, simply to pay attention to things other than life is a real killing. Apparently, we may not bring in anything of death, but we may draw people's attention away from life to many other things. Although this appears not to be death, in fact it is a real killing.

For many years I was bothered by the phrase *the letter kills*. To my realization, when I dealt with the letter, it seemed that I was not killed, and I had no intention to kill. Gradually after a long time I began to understand the proper meaning. When we say that the letter kills, it means that mere doctrine, the knowledge of the letter, causes people to pay attention to things other than life. When someone ministers, it may seem that there is nothing of death, but there may be no life there, only something other than life. We may not say that this is death, but it has nothing to do with life; it is the absence of life. Therefore, it is a killing. This is the correct meaning of *the letter kills*. The deeper meaning of this phrase is that when we deal with things or pay attention to things other than life, that is a killing.

A Personal Testimony
of Turning from the Letter to Life

In my own Christian life I have had this experience. At the very beginning of my salvation, I was very living. Immediately following a person's salvation, he is living and desires to pray and know the Word. A young brother especially likes to obtain more knowledge. Accordingly, I was brought into contact with a Brethren group which was particularly strict in the study and exposition of the Word. For seven years I studied at the feet of the Brethren teachers. I attended almost every one of their meetings during this time. I listened to more than a thousand messages concerning all the types, prophecies, and expositions of book after book of the Bible.

The Brethren spent a great deal of time studying Daniel chapters two, seven, nine, and eleven, especially the end of chapter nine concerning the seventy weeks and the second half of the last week, the last three and a half years of this age. During those seven years with the Brethren I was really "addicted" to their teachings. I could even recite what they taught word by word. Apparently there was nothing wrong and there was no death. They did not criticize others but positively passed on what they had to others. However, in those seven years I never heard a message saying that Christ is life to us and that this living Christ today dwells in us. No one would talk about this. Rather, what they always talked about were the types, prophecies, and fulfillment of the prophecies. One person among them was even a "living concordance." He could quickly tell you in what book and in what chapter any verse was located. He was very trained in the study of the letter of the Bible.

It was a great mercy of the Lord to me that after seven years with the Brethren, by the fall of 1931, I realized within me that there must be something wrong. I did not love the world; I had given that up as a young man. I also was not sinning, and I had a heart to seek after the Lord and study His Word day by day. I also went to meetings regularly, sometimes even walking through deep snow. However, I still felt dead within, and I had no fruit. For seven years I did not bring one person to the Lord. I felt weak, poor, and impotent. At this point I continued to attend their meetings, but when I rose up every morning to pray, I would go up to the mountains about ten to fifteen minutes away. I prayed to the Lord and wept, saying, "What is wrong with me, Lord?" It was in this way that after about six months, from the fall until the next spring, I broke through. At that time, I realized that all the teachings I had received were sound and scriptural, but they were killing. They had been killing me for seven years. Although I was very living when I was first saved, I had become dead after seven years; the teachings of the letter had put me to death.

Around July of 1932, after I had prayed in this way for six months, the Lord did something under His sovereignty, and I was brought into contact with Brother Watchman Nee. The Lord brought him to the city where I was living. That was the crisis, the turning point, in my life. I had no intention to stop meeting with the Brethren, but the next day after Brother Nee left, a man came to see me. He came to talk about personal things, not spiritual things, but that night the Lord brought us to the beach, and the man asked me to baptize him. That was something miraculous. I was young, and I felt that I could not do this, but he had the ground to ask me to baptize him because I had already shared many things about baptism with him. At that time I was about twenty-five years old. That was the start of the Lord's work in my hometown.

Spontaneously the Holy Spirit led us to stop attending the denominations, and we two began to meet together. Two days later, two others heard that I had baptized the first one, and they came to be baptized. Then on the third day, we baptized another two. By the Lord's Day there were seven of us, and by the next week, there were about nine. On the following Lord's Day, we began to have the Lord's table with eleven. We were eleven brothers, with no sisters, like the eleven disciples. We met in this way for three weeks, after which a sister began to meet with us. The number increased quickly, and by the end of the year nearly eighty were meeting with us. This happened because my entire being was turned from the letter to life. Even though I was young and did not know much, my messages were aggressive and challenging, and people were attracted.

By this I now realize what it means for the letter to kill. It is to pay attention to knowledge instead of life. In many seminaries and Bible colleges, the more they teach, the more they kill people by their teaching. When many young people are saved, they are living and seeking the Lord, but after entering a seminary, all day long they are under the killing of the letter of knowledge. We must learn to pay attention not to mere knowledge and letter but to spirit and life. If we pay attention to anything other than life, we will kill others. Although we have no intention to do this, we will do it unconsciously.

The letter kills, but the Spirit gives life. Therefore, we must exercise the spirit and let the Spirit take the lead. Then life will be ministered. The living letters of Christ can be composed only by the Spirit, by the ministering of life, not by knowledge, teaching, or doctrine.

BEHOLDING AND REFLECTING TO BE TRANSFORMED INTO THE IMAGE OF CHRIST

Verses 17 and 18 of chapter three say, "And the Lord is the Spirit; and where the Spirit of the Lord is, there is freedom. But we all with unveiled face, beholding and reflecting like a mirror the glory of the Lord, are being transformed into the same image from glory to glory, even as from the Lord Spirit." The better translators agree that the Greek word here for *beholding* needs another verb. Some versions use the word *beholding,* while others indicate the meaning of reflecting. However, the Greek word conveys the meaning of beholding for reflecting. Therefore, we must add a second verb, *reflecting,* so as to read "beholding to reflect" or "beholding and reflecting." If we put these two terms together, we have the proper meaning of the Greek word.

Verse 18 says that we behold and reflect not "in" a mirror but "like" a mirror, since we ourselves are the mirrors. Like mirrors, we behold and reflect with an open, unveiled face. If there is a veil covering our face, we do not have an open face, but now the veil is taken away. We have an unveiled face like a mirror without any covering that can behold its subject and reflect it. When a mirror beholds a person, that person is in the mirror, and the mirror reflects that person. There is no need to see this person directly because we can see him in the mirror; the mirror reflects him by beholding him. Formerly, the people of Israel had a veil. With us, however, the veil is now gone, so nothing covers us. We are a mirror with an unveiled, uncovered face looking at Christ and beholding Him. The more we behold Him, the more we reflect Him.

Verse 18 continues to say that we are being transformed into the image of Christ. The King James Version renders this word as *changed,* which is too poor. This is the same word translated as *transformed* in Romans 12:2. By our beholding to reflect Christ we are transformed into the same image, that is, Christ's image, from glory to glory, even as from the Lord Spirit. To begin with, there may be no image in a mirror. However, the more a mirror beholds a certain person, the more that person's image is in the mirror. In this way the mirror is transformed into that image. As the mirrors, we originally beheld something other than Christ, but that has been done away with by Christ's redemption. Now as mirrors we are free and unveiled to behold Christ, and the more we behold Christ, the more His image is impressed into us. In this way, we are transformed into the image of Christ.

The real ministry of life is to help people realize how to behold Christ in an unveiled way as the mirrors and be transformed into His image. The more we behold Him, the more we reflect Him and are transformed into His image. If a mirror beholds a person for merely half a minute, not much of that person will be reflected in the mirror. The longer we as the mirrors behold Christ, the more we are transformed into His image to become a full reflection of His image. This is not a matter of gift, teaching, or knowledge. This is a matter of the living ministry of life.

We need to be dealt with by the Lord. Then we will know how to help others to be dealt with by Him, how to put off their veils, and how to turn their heart. They will be right with Christ, and they will know how to look to Him, behold Him, and have direct fellowship with Him without any kind of frustration. They will be transformed progressively into the image of Christ to be a genuine and full reflection of Christ. This is the fruit of the work of the living ministry of life. This is a work which gifts, knowledge, and teaching can never accomplish.

This kind of work can be accomplished only by the living ministry of life, which comes from the work of the cross and from the living Christ being wrought into us. By the working of the cross and the living Christ being wrought into us, we have the ministry and we become the ministry. It is by this living ministry that people are helped to become unveiled mirrors to behold and reflect Christ and be transformed into His image. This is not merely the passing on to others of objective knowledge. It is something very living and very subjective ministered to others in spirit by the work of the cross.

THE DECAYING OF THE OUTER MAN
AND THE RENEWING OF THE INNER MAN

Verse 7 of chapter four says, "But we have this treasure in earthen vessels." No doubt, we are the earthen vessels, and the treasure within us is Christ, the embodiment of the Triune God. How can this treasure within us be prevailing, manifested, and ministered to others? There is no other way but by our brokenness through the working of the cross.

The Soul Standing with the Body or the Spirit

Verse 16 says, "Therefore we do not lose heart; but though our outer man is decaying, yet our inner man is being renewed day by day." Here is a great problem in our study of the Word: What is the outer man, and what is the inner man? We may be quick to answer that the outer man is the natural man, and the inner man is the spiritual man. However, if we answer in such a hasty way, we will make a mistake. It is not easy to expound a verse or chapter of the Scriptures, and it is easy to interpret in a loose way. The right way to expound any part of the Word is to understand its context. We need to read the entire context of 2 Corinthians 4. According to verses 10 and 11, *outer man* refers not only to the soul but even more to the body. Verse 10 says, "Always bearing about in the body the putting to death of Jesus."

Strictly speaking, the outer man in this chapter refers to the body, but it includes the soul standing with the body and controlled by the body. It is the body connected and incorporated with the soul. Under God's sovereignty our body is always put into suffering. The body together with the soul is always being consumed. Most of the sufferings of the apostle Paul were the consuming of his body. He suffered very much in his body. According to verse 9, he was "cast down but not destroyed." This means that when he was persecuted, his body was cast down, but he himself was not killed, not destroyed. All of the things mentioned in this context refer mostly to the suffering and consuming of the body. However, the soul has much to do with the body. When our body suffers, our soul also suffers. If we do not have some kind of suffering in our body, it is difficult for our soul to suffer much. The soul suffers mainly through the body's suffering.

What then is the inner man? Strictly speaking, the inner man here does not refer to the spirit alone. It refers to the soul, our inward part, with the spirit. Romans 8:6 confirms this. It says that our mind, the main part of our soul, can stand with the flesh or with the spirit. If our soul stands with the flesh, it becomes a part of the outer man. If it stands with the spirit, it becomes a part of the inner man. This is the meaning of the outer man and the inner man in 2 Corinthians 3.

Being Renewed through Sufferings

The outer man is the body with the soul. This has to be consumed. The inner man is the soul with the spirit, and this has to be renewed. By our experience we can realize this. When we are suffering, perhaps from a certain kind of sickness, this is a suffering through the body. At this time, however, not only our body is consumed, but our soul is also consumed, while at the same time, our soul is revived with our spirit. Before the time of suffering, our soul was very much involved with our body. However, after a period of suffering, our soul turns much to the spirit. The relationship between the soul and the body is consumed, and the relationship between the soul and the spirit is revived and renewed.

If persecutors beat us and put us into prison, we will no doubt suffer in our body. At the same time, our soul which is related to the body, will also suffer. If our soul were not related to our body, it would not suffer when the body suffers. Our soul suffers when our body suffers because the two are "married." Because our soul is related to the body, the Lord raises up suffering for our body in order to turn our soul away from the body to the spirit. Therefore, after our sickness or imprisonment, that is, after our suffering in the body, the result is that the soul turns away from the body to the spirit and is transformed. It is purified from a relationship with the body and brought into a revived and renewed relationship with the spirit. Then our mind, will, and emotion are revived, strengthened, and renewed spiritually.

Before we suffer, our soul is too attached to the body and too much for the body as a part of the outer man. Therefore, the Lord needs to deal with the outer man to cause the outer man to suffer, that is, to be consumed. The more the outer man is consumed, the more our soul turns away from the flesh to the spirit. On the other hand, the soul is renewed and revived with the spirit. This is the proper meaning of decaying and renewing in verse 16. Then our soul will not be so attached to the body, that is, to the flesh. Our soul will be purified, adjusted, renewed, and turned to the spirit to cooperate with the spirit and be incorporated with the spirit. This renewed soul—the renewed mind, will, and emotion—is suitable to express Christ for the spirit. Once again, this is a word not of gift or knowledge but of a living ministry.

The Work of the Ministry Being to Turn Our Soul from the Body to the Spirit

The soul of an unbeliever is one hundred percent on the side of his body. Not one bit of his soul is turned to his spirit.

The soul of a young believer in Christ is also very much on the side of his body. Although he loves the Lord, his soul is not much incorporated with the spirit. How much of our own soul is attached to our flesh, and how much does our soul stand with our spirit? We spend too much time with the flesh and very little with the spirit. In what way can our soul turn from the flesh to the spirit? It is not by teaching but by suffering. Teaching is not adequate to turn our soul from the body to the spirit. Teaching can cause us to understand, but it does not bring us into the reality.

The more a brother or sister suffers physically and materially, the more his or her soul progressively turns from the side of the flesh to the spirit. This means that the outer man is being consumed and the inner man is being renewed. I have seen many dear brothers and sisters who were strong persons prior to their suffering. They were strong in the body and in the flesh. Then the Lord put them into a situation of sickness, and they suffered physically for many years. Gradually, the more they suffered physically, the more their mind, will, and emotion were turned from the body to the spirit. Eventually, such persons who have been suffering physically for a long time become very spiritual. Their mind, emotion, and will are very much on the side of the spirit instead of on the side of the flesh. This indicates that the outer man is consumed and the inner man is renewed. It is in this way that the Lord deals with our soul. Suffering turns our soul from the body to the spirit. This is the work of the ministry.

MINISTERS OF GOD BY THE WORKING OF THE CROSS

Being Wrought with the Lord and Knowing Him

Chapter six stresses the working of the cross and Christ being wrought into us. Verse 4 says, "But in everything we commend ourselves as ministers of God." In other books written by the apostle Paul, he called himself a servant or slave, but in this book he uses mostly the word *minister*. In the Greek text, the words *slave* and *minister* are different. The word *slave* has a particular background. At that time around the Mediterranean Sea there was a custom that one could be sold to a master to be a bondman, someone without any freedom. This was Paul's meaning when he used the word *slave*. The apostles were the Lord's slaves. The word *minister,* on the other hand, means that something of the Lord has been wrought into someone to make him the minister of the Lord.

Someone may be a person's slave but not be a good minister to him. To be a slave means that he has no liberty. He has been sold to another, he has no rights, and he submits to his master. However, it is very possible that he may not know anything about his master. He may know how to submit to him, but he does not know what his master intends to do and what his thoughts and desires are. Then, although he may be a good slave, he is not a good minister. In order to be a minister and deal with people on behalf of his master, a person must be wrought by his master. The master's heart, desire, intention, thought, and relationships with others must be clear to that person. Then he can go to others as a minister representing his master and speaking exactly according to him.

We can see this in diplomatic affairs. The foreign minister of a country, such as the American ambassador to China, must be a man who knows the affairs of his government. If someone knows his government's intention, purpose, policy, desire, and relationship with other nations, he can be the proper representative to another country. However, if someone is a citizen of a country yet does not know anything about his government's affairs, he can never be a minister of his country. In the same way, if something of the Lord has been wrought into a servant of the Lord, he becomes a minister of the Lord.

In 2 Corinthians the term *minister* is used more than in other books because in this book the servants of the Lord are wrought by the Lord. Something of the Lord's character, life, intention, desire, and purpose has been wrought into them to make them the ministers of Christ.

Becoming the Ministers of Christ
through Sufferings and the Experience of Grace

The ministers of the new covenant are described in verses 4 through 10, which say, "But in everything we commend ourselves as ministers of God, in much endurance, in afflicTions, in necessities, in distresses, in stripes, in imprisonments, in tumults, in labors, in watchings, in fastings; in pureness, in knowledge, in long-suffering, in kindness, in a holy spirit, in unfeigned love, in the word of truth, in the power of God; through the weapons of righteousness on the right and on the left, through glory and dishonor, through evil report and good report; as deceivers and yet true; as unknown and yet well known; as dying and yet behold we live; as being disciplined and yet not being put to death; as made sorrowful yet always rejoicing; as poor yet enriching many; as having nothing and yet possessing all things."

Verse 8 speaks of evil report. Many times the evil reports actually comfort us. We should not think that because we are faithful to the Lord that we will always receive good reports. There may be many evil reports about us. Even the apostle Paul suffered many evil reports about himself. Verse 8 also says that the ministers were considered as deceivers. If we are faithful to the Lord, many times people will say that we are deceivers. Only when we are not faithful to the Lord will everyone praise us as being honest. However, that kind of honesty is not the real honesty; it is a diplomatic honesty.

Chapter eleven again speaks of the sufferings and the working of the cross upon the ministers of the Lord. In verses 23 through 29 Paul says, "Ministers of Christ are they? I speak as being beside myself, I more so! In labors more abundantly, in imprisonments more abundantly, in stripes excessively, in deaths often. Under the hands of the Jews five times I received forty stripes less one; three times I was beaten with rods, once I was stoned, three times I was shipwrecked, a night and a day I have spent in the deep; in journeys often, in dangers of rivers, in dangers of robbers, in dangers from my race, in dangers from the Gentiles, in dangers in the city, in dangers in the wilderness, in dangers in the sea, in dangers among false brothers; in labor and hardship; in watchings often; in hunger and thirst; in fastings often; in cold and nakedness—apart from the things which have not been mentioned, there is this: the crowd of cares pressing upon me daily, the anxious concern for all the churches. Who is weak, and I am not weak? Who is stumbled, and I myself do not burn?" Here we see a suffering person. The ministry comes out of this kind of suffering.

Verse 7 of chapter twelve says, "And because of the transcendence of the revelations, in order that I might not be exceedingly lifted up, there was given to me a thorn in the flesh, a messenger of Satan, that he might buffet me, in order that I might not be exceedingly lifted up." The Lord knew that even the apostle Paul could be proud and lifted up, so he gave him a thorn in the flesh. *In the flesh* here refers to the physical sufferings in the body. Verses 8 and 9 continue, "Concerning this I entreated the Lord three times that it might depart from me. And He has said to me, My grace is sufficient for you, for My power is perfected in weakness. Most gladly therefore I will rather boast in my weaknesses that the power of Christ might tabernacle over me." The Lord would not answer Paul's entreaty to take away the thorn. Instead, the Lord left the thorn there to create an opportunity for Paul to experience more and more of His grace.

Verse 10 says, "Therefore I am well pleased in weaknesses, in insults, in necessities, in persecutions and distresses, on behalf of Christ; for when I am weak, then I am powerful." This is the description of a minister and the ministry. The ministry comes out of suffering and from the real experience of the Lord Himself as grace. The strength and the power is the Lord Himself experienced by us and becoming our grace.

MINISTERS OF THE TRIUNE GOD

The book of 2 Corinthians concludes with, "The grace of the Lord Jesus Christ and the love of God and the fellowship of the Holy Spirit be with you all" (13:14). This is to say, the Triune God be with you all. Love is the source of grace; grace is the expression, the emergence, of love; and fellowship is the transmission of this grace to us. The love is in the grace, and the grace is in the fellowship. Moreover, the fellowship is of the Holy Spirit. When we have the fellowship of the Holy Spirit, we enjoy the grace of Christ, and when we enjoy the grace of Christ, we have the love of God. This means that the Triune God has been wrought into us, and we are one with the Triune God. As such, we become the ministers of the Triune God with the ministry of the Triune God. We have not merely a gift but the ministry of the Triune God, and we minister the Triune God to others. This is a sketch of the book of 2 Corinthians.

CHAPTER FIFTEEN

WALKING BY THE SPIRIT
IN GALATIANS

Scripture Reading: Gal. 3:16, 29; 5:16-17, 22, 25

In the order and the arrangement of the books of the New Testament, there is the sovereignty of the Lord. It is appropriate to have 1 and 2 Corinthians follow Romans. The two Epistles to the Corinthians show us that the Christian walk and the church life are a matter not of gifts or knowledge but of Christ being wrought into us by the working of the cross. They deal with gifts and knowledge on the negative side and with the living Christ working within us through His cross on the positive side. This is the central thought of these two books. Then following 1 and 2 Corinthians, we have Galatians. This is the right order.

THE PROBLEM
OF THE LAW AND JUDAISM

In the realm of religion, the law is a prevailing problem. For thousands of years of human civilization, there has never been anything as prevailing and prominent as the law given to man. Among the human race, many philosophies and ethical systems have been invented. According to the human thought, not only philosophy and ethics but also certain religions formed among people are helpful to some extent. The most outstanding item in this realm is the law given to man by God. This is a significant matter. Among all the races in human civilization, the law given by God is the greatest item. It is greater than all the other human elements. It is greater, better, and higher than all philosophies and teachings of ethics and all forms of religion on the earth.

Based upon the law given by God, the Jewish religion was formed. Judaism is the highest and the most genuine religion. However, Christ has now come, and the church has come into existence. Now in the universe, particularly on this earth, there is the universal man. How can the law given by God with the Jewish religion based on this law coexist with Christ and the church? How can we have the law with its religion together with this universal man? Are these two contradictory to one another, or can these two be reconciled? This was the first and greatest problem that the church faced. Immediately after the birth of the church, the church faced its biggest problem, the law and its religion. Judaism and the law were the biggest deterring factors to the building up of the church. Therefore, after Paul's two Epistles to the Corinthians, Galatians deals with this matter of the law. We need to be very impressed with the matter of the law. We must understand where the law stands in relation to God's economy. We must know what kind of position God has given the law and what the function and purpose of the law are.

THE POSITION OF THE LAW

The Jewish people believe that besides God nothing is as great as the law. Only God Himself is higher and greater than the law. In their understanding they give all the ground to the law; it is second only to God Himself. Now we ourselves must deal with the problem of the law. In our understanding and according to God's revelation, what is the position assigned by God to the law?

Being a Slave
as a Child-Conductor

The law is no longer the most important item. Galatians 3:24 says that the law is our child-conductor unto Christ. The King James Version mistakenly translates this word as *schoolmaster*. Strictly speaking, the law is not a schoolmaster but a child-conductor. Conybeare tells us that in the ancient times there was not the system of schooling that we have today. At that time there were schoolmasters, to whose houses parents would send their young children. The more wealthy people at that time had slaves, so when parents sent their children to the schoolmaster's home to study, a slave would accompany them. Since the children were young, they could get lost travelling from their parent's home to the schoolmaster, so they needed the slave to care for them. Certain versions of the Bible mistakenly cause people to understand that the law is the schoolmaster. The law is not the schoolmaster; the schoolmaster is Christ, and the law is the child-conductor. God's intention is to bring us to Christ. However, just as parents used slaves to bring young, immature children to a schoolmaster, God used the law as a child-conductor to bring His people to Christ, the schoolmaster. Because children are young, foolish, and childish, they need a child-conductor. However, when they grow up, there is no need of a child-conductor. Hence, according to the context of Galatians 3, the position of the law is the position of a slave.

Being a Maidservant

Galatians 4:21-31 shows us something more concerning the position of the law. Abraham had two wives. Sarah is a type of God's grace, while Abraham's maidservant, Hagar, typifies the law. The position of the law is the position of a maidservant, or concubine. Therefore, the position of the law is not positive. None of us would want to be the child of a concubine.

For this reason we know that the law is not something according to God's final goal. The law helped toward the goal, but it does not belong to God's ultimate purpose. Galatians 3:19 tells us that the law "was added because of the transgressions," but it was not something originally intended by God. The law was not part of God's original purpose, and it is not a part of His ultimate purpose, His ultimate consummation. Rather, it was added on the way. During the process of fulfilling God's eternal purpose, something happened, so the law was added to correct and adjust the situation. We must be very clear about this.

THE PURPOSE OF THE LAW

God's Original Purpose and Ultimate Intention to Give Us Christ

The book of Galatians reveals that the original purpose and ultimate intention of God is to give us Christ. God's plan and God's purpose is to give us Christ as everything. At the time of Abraham, God came in to promise him not the law and not seeds but a seed. That promise to Abraham is called the gospel in Galatians 3:8. Verse 8 says, "And the Scripture, foreseeing that God would justify the Gentiles out of faith, announced the gospel beforehand to Abraham: 'In you shall all the nations be blessed.'" We may have thought that gospel preaching started after the Lord ascended to the heavens. However, according to Galatians 3 God began to preach the gospel to mankind at least in Genesis 12 when He promised Abraham a seed. The message of the gospel is, "In you shall all the nations be blessed," and the content of this message is, "your seed, who is Christ." Verse 16 says, "But to Abraham were the promises spoken and to his seed. He does not say, 'And to the seeds,' as concerning many, but as concerning one: 'And to your seed,' who is Christ." God preached the gospel to Abraham, and its message was that all the nations would be blessed in him. The content of the message is that Christ is the unique seed because God's intention and purpose is to give us Christ as everything.

At a certain point in time, before the fullness of the time (4:4), God came in to promise that He would give a seed, Christ. We must realize who this Christ is. Christ is all-inclusive. He is the very embodiment of God; all the fullness of the Godhead dwells in Him (Col. 2:9). He is the very reality of God; all that God is, all God's fullness, is embodied in Him. Christ is such a One, yet He became the seed of Abraham. Therefore, He is a man. On the one hand, Christ as the seed is a blessing, and on the other hand, this seed is the one who inherits the blessing (Gal. 3:8-9, 14, 16). Moreover, He is the one who blesses. He is the very God who blesses, He is the promised blessing, and He is the seed who inherits the blessing. This is altogether wonderful! If we want to have a share in this blessing, we must be in Christ. In principle, God does not bless you or me; He blesses only one person, who is the seed. If we desire to receive the blessing, we must be a part of this one seed. We must be in Christ, be a part of Christ, and belong to Christ.

Galatians 3:29 says, "And if you are of Christ, then you are Abraham's seed, heirs according to promise." The word *seed* is singular; the descendants of Abraham are many, but they are in Christ. You and I must be in Christ. Christ is everything. He is the one who blesses, the promised blessing, and the One who inherits the blessing.

The Law Conducting Us to Christ

What then is the function of the law? Before the children arrive at the home of the schoolmaster, they need the care of a child-conductor. In the same way, before we came to Christ, there was the need of the law to conduct us, to protect us, to keep us from going astray, and to bring us to Christ. This is the position and the function of the law. God has no intention to ask us to keep the law. He knows already that we cannot keep the law. On the contrary, God's intention in giving us the law is that we will break the law in order to prove that we are sinful and that we need Christ.

However, even such a good thing as the law was utilized by the enemy, Satan, to frustrate God's people from contacting Christ. This was the subtlety of the enemy. Parents used a child-conductor to lead the children to the schoolmaster, but the enemy used the child-conductor to keep the children away from the schoolmaster. This was exactly what Satan did in the early days of the church. The Judaizers, those Jews who were so much for Judaism, stressed the law to such an extent that it substituted for Christ. Through the Judaizers Satan utilized the law to distract God's people from Christ.

This is the reason that the book of Galatians was written. It was written with the purpose to make us clear that the law is not God's ultimate intention, and it is not something of God's original plan. The law was something added on the way for a certain purpose. Since the Christ of God has come, we are now in the schoolmaster's house, and we are even one with the schoolmaster. Therefore, we no longer need the law. The law is over; we must drop the law, forget about the law, give up the law, and put the law aside. Paul wrote this book to the Galatians in order to tell them that they no longer needed the law, the child-conductor, because the schoolmaster is here, and we are one with the schoolmaster. Just as Hagar, the concubine, and her son had to be cast away, so the law has to be cast away (4:30). What we need is to stay with Christ as the schoolmaster, enjoy what is in Him, and be one with Him. If we understand this short word, we can understand the book of Galatians.

ENJOYING CHRIST BY THE SPIRIT

After I was saved, I paid much attention to the books of Romans and Galatians. I spent nearly all that I had to buy some books to help explain them. I was told that the best exposition on Galatians was the one written by Martin Luther. I obtained a copy, and I looked into it. However, Luther's exposition on Galatians speaks mainly of justification by faith. It says little about Christ as everything to us. I read the six chapters of Galatians again and again, but I could not understand them. I could recite nearly every verse in this book, but I could not understand what Paul was talking about.

In recent years the Lord opened my eyes and showed me that Galatians can be summed up in five words: the law and Christ, the cross, and the flesh and the Spirit. The law is versus Christ, substituting for Christ, and the flesh, the self, is versus the Spirit. God's intention is that we enjoy Christ, have Christ, experience Christ, and live out Christ by and in the Spirit. However, our foolishness according to our concept causes us to try to keep the law by ourselves, that is, by the flesh. Therefore, the law is contradictory to Christ. In the same way, the flesh, the self, opposes the Spirit. If we are in the Spirit, then Christ is everything to us, but if we are in our self, our flesh, we will try to keep the law.

The flesh is related to the law, while the Spirit is the very element of Christ. Now the cross of Christ has come in to put the flesh and self to death and to free us from the law

(2:19-20; 5:24). Negatively speaking, we are dead and have nothing to do with the law, and on the positive side, the cross brings us into the Spirit. When we are in the Spirit, we have Christ as our life, we enjoy Christ as everything, we experience Christ, and we live out Christ. This causes the growth in life. We must keep in mind the five key terms of this book: the law, Christ, the flesh, the Spirit, and the cross. Everything that this book speaks about is contained within these five terms.

CHRIST VERSUS RELIGION

The central thought of the first chapter of Galatians is the contrast between religion and Christ. If we keep this in mind, we will know the proper meaning of this chapter. The apostle Paul presented himself as an example to illustrate this. Formerly, he was very involved with the Jewish religion. He was trained in Judaism and learned it thoroughly. Not only so, he was zealous for it and gave himself entirely to it. This is man's way. However, one day God came in and revealed not a religion, a system, a set of forms, teachings, or practices but a person in him (v. 16). Although Paul was zealous for his forefathers' religion and was one hundred percent for it, God revealed Christ in him. Then Christ became everything to him. Christ became life, revelation, and vision within him, and He became the preaching, the work, and the activity outside of him. Moreover, the gospel of the living person of Christ realized and experienced by Paul was not taught to him by man but was a revelation by Jesus Christ (vv. 11-12).

CRUCIFIED WITH CHRIST

In the second chapter, Paul, an experienced believer, told us that he is crucified with Christ; therefore, he has been set free from the law and is dead to the law (vv. 19-21). He has nothing to do with the law, since it is no more he who lives but Christ who lives in him. He is no longer obligated to the law or tied to the law. Now he needs only to cooperate with this living person.

THE PROMISED SEED—CHRIST

In order to understand Galatians 3, we must get into the key thought. The Judaizers thought that the law was the primary item that God gave to them. However, Paul, the writer of this book, proved to them that the primary item given by God is not the law but His promise. The promise which God gave to Abraham is a seed, which is the very God incarnated to be a man (v. 16). In Him, that is, in this very seed, God will be the blessing and the portion to all the nations. Moreover, the seed as the blessing can be possessed, realized, and experienced only by the Spirit (v. 14). We must have the Spirit and be in the Spirit in order to receive the blessing. God is in Christ, Christ is the Spirit, and the Spirit is the witness, the reality. If we receive the Spirit, we have Christ and we have God in Christ.

The key thought in this chapter is that God's intention is to make Himself our portion, our blessing, in Christ by the Spirit. God's intention is not the law; the law was added on the way. We must be in Christ, and we must be in the Spirit. We must receive the Spirit to enjoy Christ as everything, to be in Christ, to be one with Him, and to be of Christ. Now we are of the one seed, and this one seed is everything to us (vv. 16, 29). Chapter three reveals that it is not a matter of keeping the law by ourselves, but a matter of being in Christ by the Spirit. By the Spirit we enjoy, experience, realize, and possess Christ as everything to us.

THE SONSHIP

Galatians 4 tells us that now we are no more little children (vv. 1-3). Rather, as those who have been brought to the schoolmaster, we are in Him, and He is in us. Now we are not merely children but sons and heirs (vv. 5-7). We have not only the life of the children but the sonship. The sonship mentioned in this chapter is extraordinary. According to the custom of the ancient Roman Empire, a son obtained the right of inheritance. This is the meaning of sonship. Before maturity, however, the son was a son only; he did not yet have the sonship. Before a person is twenty-one years old, he is the son of his father with the life of a son, but he does not have the right of the son, that is, the sonship. He does not have the right to inherit all that his father has until he is fully grown. One day the father will declare that he is not only a son but also that he has the sonship with the full right to inherit everything of the father.

The apostle's thought in this chapter is that from the time that Christ came and accomplished His work, we are no more underage. This is not according to anything we have done but according to what Christ accomplished. Because we are no longer underage minors but grown children, God gives us the sonship. Now we can inherit whatever God is. This inheritance is the fullness of the Godhead, which is Christ Himself. Because we are full-grown ones, sons who are of age, we are entitled to the sonship to inherit whatever Christ is. Formerly, we were children under the hand of a slave, a child-conductor. As such, we could not enjoy all that the schoolmaster had. Now, however, we have been transferred out of the child-conductor's hand unto the schoolmaster. We have come of age and have received the sonship, the right of inheritance. This inheritance is nothing less than Christ Himself with all the fullness of the Godhead. Therefore, we must be filled; that is, the fullness of the Godhead in Christ has to be formed in us (v. 19). Whatever Christ is and whatever Christ has must be formed in us. That we are filled in this way proves that we are the sons of God.

LIVING IN SPIRIT AND WALKING BY THE SPIRIT

Galatians 5 tells us that since Christ has set us free from the law and has made us one with Him, we should not go back to the law (v. 1). If we return to the law, then Christ will profit us nothing, and we will be brought to nought, separated from Christ (vv. 2, 4). Rather, we must now live by the Spirit and walk by the Spirit (vv. 16, 25). When we live and walk by the Spirit, the flesh and the self are put away. Although the self and the flesh have been dealt with already on the cross of Christ, this has to be applied and experienced by us. When we live and walk by the Spirit, our self and flesh are put away in our practical experience.

In this chapter the phrase *by the Spirit* is a problem to the readers because there is no definite article in the Greek (vv. 5, 16, 18, 25). It is difficult for translators to decide whether these portions refer to the Holy Spirit or to our human spirit. Galatians 5:16 says, "Walk by the Spirit," but the Greek text may be simply rendered, "Walk by spirit." Verse 17 says, "The flesh lusts against the Spirit," and verse 22 speaks of "the fruit of the Spirit," both using the definite article. Although these verses contain the same grammatical construction, some versions render *spirit* in the former and *Spirit* in the latter. Moreover, verse 25 does not have the definite article, yet many versions render the word as *Spirit*. With or without the definite article, the same word may be rendered as *spirit* or *Spirit*.

In addition, the term *Holy Spirit* is not used in this chapter; in each case it is only a form of the word *pneuma*. This simply shows us that the Spirit of God is one with our human spirit, and to live in our spirit is to live in the Spirit. We are one spirit with the Lord; the Spirit and our spirit mingle as one spirit. To walk in the Spirit or to walk in spirit means the same thing; it means that we live and walk in our human spirit mingled with the Spirit, or we may say, in the Spirit who mingles Himself with our spirit.

Now we can realize that the Christian walk is a matter of living and walking by the Spirit. Therefore, we must learn how to exercise our spirit; this is the key and the secret. As we have seen, God's intention is that Christ be everything to us, and Christ is in us, that is, in our spirit. What we must do now is live and walk by the Spirit. Hence, we must know how to exercise our spirit. Then we will have the practical experience of Christ in our daily walk.

THE WORLD CRUCIFIED TO US AND WE TO THE WORLD

Chapter six is simple. It reveals mainly that the world has been crucified to us and we to the world (v. 14). We have been crucified, and we are on the cross. Therefore, the cross of Christ is our ground. Moreover, because of the cross the whole world, including the law and Judaism, has been crucified. *The world* in verse 14 includes everything on the earth involving the human race, but in the thought of the writer, the world especially includes Judaism with the law. We know this because 1:4 contains the same thought, saying, "Who gave Himself for our sins that He might rescue us out of the present evil age." The Greek word here is not *kosmos,* meaning *world,* but *aionos,* meaning *age.* The world as a whole is composed of many ages, and each age is the part of the world which we contact at the present. The present evil age at the apostle's time was mainly Judaism. Therefore, to be delivered from the present age at the apostle's time means to be delivered from Judaism, although in principle the age includes everything of the world.

As far as we are concerned, because of the cross the whole world, including Judaism and the law, is crucified. On the other hand, as far as the world is concerned, we are crucified. Therefore, we and the world have nothing to do with one another because between us two there is the cross. Our position is the cross. Therefore, in our life, living, and daily walk, we know nothing of circumcision or uncircumcision; we only know one thing—to be a new creation (6:15). Circumcision and uncircumcision are matters belonging to the old creation, but now we are a new creation. Paul knew nothing of these matters. He did not want to bear the signs of the law upon him. Instead, he bore in his body the brands of Jesus (v. 17).

THE GRACE OF OUR LORD JESUS CHRIST
WITH OUR SPIRIT

The last verse in chapter six says, "The grace of our Lord Jesus Christ be with your spirit, brothers. Amen" (v. 18). The closing word, the conclusion, of Galatians is that we must know two things—grace and our spirit. How regrettable today that Christians know nearly nothing about grace and our spirit. In today's Christianity it is difficult to hear any messages on these two matters. Grace in our spirit is nothing less than God in Christ as the Spirit. Any other definition of grace is meaningless. The grace in verse 18 is a grace that is in us, even in our spirit. What else can be in our spirit? We may say that grace is something of the Holy Spirit, that the Holy Spirit strengthens, tempers, enlightens, guides, leads, and teaches us in our spirit, but this is too shallow. Eventually we have to say that this guiding, leading, enlightening, strengthening, helping, and speaking Spirit is the grace Himself. Grace in our spirit is nothing less than the Triune God—God Himself in Christ as the Spirit—enjoyed by us daily, hourly, and moment by moment. It is the gracious God in His Son by the Spirit to be enjoyed by us as our comfort, our strength, our peace, our might, and as everything to us. There is no better definition for grace than this.

We must know this grace, and we must know how to exercise our spirit because this wonderful grace is in our spirit. Therefore, we must learn how to discern our soul from our spirit (Heb. 4:12). If we do not know how to discern our spirit, we are like the children of Israel who wandered in the wilderness. The book of Hebrews speaks of the temple with its three parts—the outer court, the Holy Place, and the Holy of Holies. Our body corresponds to the outer court, our soul to the Holy Place, and our spirit to the Holy of Holies. Similarly, Egypt, the wilderness, and the good land of Canaan correspond to our body, soul, and spirit respectively. To enjoy Christ as the Passover in Egypt was similar to enjoying the sin offerings on the altar in the outer court. Those who left Egypt and came into the wilderness typify people in the soul. Those who wandered in the wilderness enjoyed the manna and the living water from the cleft rock; that is, they enjoyed a certain amount of God's presence, as the priests did in the Holy Place. This corresponds to the Christians today who are in the soul, the soulish Christians. Hebrews encourages us to press on to enter the good land. This is to enter into the Holy of Holies. We can enter into the Holy of Holies in a practical way by discerning our soul from our spirit. When we enter into our spirit, we enjoy the good land.

CHAPTER SIXTEEN

ASPECTS OF THE CHURCH IN EPHESIANS

Scripture Reading: Eph. 1:17; 3:11; 1:9-10; 3:2, 9; 4:4-6; 3:14-19; 1:22b-23; 2:15-16; 4:22-24; 5:25, 32; 2:20-22

Ephesians is the most complete book revealing the church, the Body of the universal man. All Bible students know that this book is about the church. What is revealed and mentioned in Ephesians is a deep matter. The thoughts contained in it are the deepest thoughts in the New Testament. Nearly all the main points in this book are beyond our concept. In our natural concept we do not have the kind of thoughts revealed here. It is easy to have certain concepts about religion, morality, and doing good. We may easily have thoughts about certain doctrines, teachings, knowledge, work, and service. Our minds are busy with these thoughts because these things are so familiar to the natural mentality. However, this book contains something that is one hundred percent different from all these things.

A SPIRIT OF WISDOM AND REVELATION

Therefore, in order to understand this book, we need spiritual revelation. This is why in the first chapter of this book, at the very outset, the writer offers a prayer asking that the Lord would grant us a spirit of wisdom and revelation that we may fully know not religious things, moral things, or mere doctrines and teachings but the things of God's eternal purpose (1:17). Please notice that the spirit mentioned in this prayer, strictly speaking, is not the Holy Spirit. Today Christians talk much about the Holy Spirit but almost entirely neglect the human spirit.

We need not only the Holy Spirit; even more we need our

human spirit which is able to cooperate with the Holy Spirit. We may illustrate this with sunshine and electricity. The sun may shine brightly, but what we need is a clear window to receive the sunlight. The sunshine itself is no problem, but there may be a problem with the window. Likewise, there may be no problem with the electricity, but there may be a problem with the light bulb. Although electricity is installed in a building, we still need a proper light bulb. Without the proper bulb to cooperate with the electricity, the electricity cannot be applied to perform its function. After the day of resurrection and the day of Pentecost, the Holy Spirit in all His aspects was given to the believers. He was imparted into the church and poured out upon the church. Therefore, with the Holy Spirit there is no problem. The only need is with us, and this need is a matter of our spirit. However, we may pay much attention to the Holy Spirit while neglecting our human spirit, which is where the real need is.

Ephesians 1:17 says, "That the God of our Lord Jesus Christ, the Father of glory, may give to you a spirit of wisdom and revelation in the full knowledge of Him." It is very good that many versions of the Bible use the word *spirit* here without capitalizing it. It is difficult to discern whether the word *spirit* in passages such as this one refers to the human spirit or the Holy Spirit, but in this passage it refers to our spirit more than the Holy Spirit. We need a spirit, not only a heart, of wisdom and revelation. In order to understand the book of Ephesians, our mind is of secondary importance. The primary matter is that we need a spirit of wisdom and revelation. Therefore, we should know the difference between the spirit and the heart, and we should try to exercise our spirit that it may be strengthened, clean, alert, and one of wisdom and revelation. Then we can realize the things revealed in this book in a spiritual way, not in a religious, moral, or ethical way or merely in the way of knowledge.

I hate to see that Christians know the Scriptures merely in the way of ethics. The disciples of Confucius always take the way of ethics to understand religious books. Even when the holy Scriptures come into their hands, they understand them in an ethical way. Today, many regenerated Christians try to do the same thing. In order to know the Scriptures we need to be delivered from this way. Our understanding and realization must be delivered from understanding the Scriptures in the way of ethics. The way of ethics belongs one hundred percent to the tree of the knowledge of good and evil, not to the tree of life. Rather, we must have a spirit of wisdom and revelation. A spirit of wisdom and revelation is related to the tree of life.

In order to realize something from the book of Ephesians, we must exercise our spirit. We must forget about our natural mentality, natural concepts, mere doctrines and teachings, our religious understanding, and the way of ethics. If we give up all these things, it will be easy to have a spirit of wisdom and revelation. Then we will see the things concerning God's purpose in God's light. We will understand the things mentioned in this book in an accurate way.

GOD'S ETERNAL PURPOSE AND ECONOMY

The best way to realize the sketch of Ephesians is to identify its main points. First, this book reveals God's eternal purpose. Many Christians have never noticed that in the New Testament there is such a special term, *the eternal purpose.* Even after I had been a Christian for nearly fifteen years and had studied the New Testament and read the book of Ephesians many times, I did not yet see this matter of God's eternal purpose.

Ephesians 3:11 says, "According to the eternal purpose which He made in Christ Jesus our Lord." The word *eternal* in Greek is derived from *aion,* meaning *of the ages,* that is, *eternal.* Ephesians speaks of the eternal purpose, and here *purpose* equals *plan;* both terms are correct and meaningful. Therefore, we may speak of the eternal plan which God planned in Christ. Verses 9 and 10 of chapter one also refer to the divine plan, the eternal purpose. Why is this plan called the eternal purpose? It is because this purpose was planned in eternity past and for eternity future. Therefore, it is the purpose of eternity, that is, the purpose of the ages. However, it must be accomplished in time. Between the two ends of eternity there is an interval, which is the bridge of time. Time bridges the two ends of eternity, and upon this bridge there is a process in which God's purpose is accomplished. God's purpose in eternity past and for eternity future is now being completed on this bridge of time.

Ephesians also uses the term *economy*. Ephesians 1:10 says, "Unto the economy of the fullness of the times." In the King James Version this word is translated as *dispensation*. However, it does not refer to a period of time. It refers to a way of dispensing, thus an arrangement or management. In different translations this word is rendered *dispensation, arrangement, administration, stewardship,* or *government,* but the best word is *economy*. Because God has an eternal plan, He needs an economy, a dispensation, arrangement, administration, stewardship, and government.

In chapter three the same Greek word is used twice. Verse 2 says, "If indeed you have heard of the stewardship of the grace of God which was given to me for you." The grace of God may be compared to the capital in a business. In order to fulfill God's plan, God has an operation, and the grace of God is the spiritual and divine capital in God's operation. Just as a corporation needs an economy for its capital, God's operation requires an economy, a stewardship.

Ephesians 3:9 says, "And to enlighten all that they may see what the economy of the mystery is, which throughout the ages has been hidden in God, who created all things." The King James Version follows a less trustworthy manuscript to translate *economy* as *fellowship*. According to the better manuscripts, the Greek word here is *economy*.

THE GOAL OF GOD'S ETERNAL PURPOSE

The second main point in Ephesians is the aim, the goal, of God's eternal purpose. The church is a great matter; it was planned by God, and strictly speaking it is the very economy of God for His plan. God's economy is wholly related to the church. What God planned and what He is operating to carry out is the church, so the church is the very center of God's economy. This is the reason that this book particularly speaks of the eternal purpose of God and the economy of God's grace. In order to understand the church, we must realize that it is the center of God's plan and the very substance of His economy.

We may say that the aim of God's eternal purpose is to have the church, but this is too general. If we study Ephesians with a spirit of revelation, we will realize that the aim of God's plan is to have an expression of Himself in Christ the Son by the Spirit through a Body composed and built up with many regenerated and transformed people by the mingling of Himself with humanity. If we read Ephesians with the foregoing sentence in view, we will see exactly what is in this book.

The Triune God in Ephesians

In no other book is the Triune God revealed as much as in Ephesians. Of course, we do not have here the word *Trinity,* but we have the reality, the fact, of the Divine Trinity. Of the seven "ones" in chapter four, three relate to the Three of the Divine Trinity. Verses 4-6 say, "One Spirit...one Lord...one God and Father." There are other passages in this book that contain the thought of the Divine Trinity. Verse 3 of chapter one says, "Blessed be the God and Father of our Lord Jesus Christ, who has blessed us with every spiritual blessing in the heavenlies in Christ." This verse speaks of the Father and Christ the Son. In addition, *every spiritual blessing* is related to the Holy Spirit. Therefore, this verse speaks of the Three of the Godhead.

In chapter three Paul says, "For this cause I bow my knees unto the Father, of whom every family in the heavens and on earth is named, that He would grant you, according to the riches of His glory, to be strengthened with power through His Spirit into the inner man, that Christ may make His home in your hearts through faith, that you, being rooted and grounded in love, may be full of strength to apprehend with all the saints what the breadth and length and height and depth are and to know the knowledge-surpassing love of Christ, that you may be filled unto all the fullness of God" (vv. 14-19). These verses once again mention the Three of the Divine Trinity—the Father, the Son, and the Spirit—yet They are one God. The Three work together to cause us to realize the fullness of this one God. The Father is the source, the fountain, from whom all the families in the heavens and on earth are named; the Spirit is the working means; and the Son is the very object for whom the Father planned and the Spirit works. These Three cooperate with one another for us to realize the fullness of God, that is, to make the fullness of God one with us. In this way, these verses show us the Divine Trinity.

The Triune God Being for Our Experience

There is no need for us to know the Divine Trinity for the purpose of mere doctrine and knowledge. Rather, the Divine Trinity is for our experience, that we may realize the fullness of the Godhead. Verses 14 through 19 tell us that the Father grants us to be strengthened through His Spirit. The issue of this is that Christ, the very central One, may make His home in our heart by the working of the Spirit according to what the Father planned. Then the fullness of God becomes our experience; that is, we are filled unto all the fullness of the Triune God, the fullness of the Godhead. Therefore, the Divine Trinity is a matter of experience, not a matter of doctrine. In doctrine we can never understand the Divine Trinity in a proper way. Moreover, no one can explain the Divine Trinity. How can we say that the Three are one God? Whenever the Scripture mentions the Divine Trinity, it is for our experience.

Matthew 28:19 tells us to baptize people into the name, not into the names, of the Father and of the Son and of the Holy Spirit. To baptize the repenting and believing ones is to cause them to experience the Divine Trinity. Similarly, 2 Corinthians 13:14 says, "The grace of the Lord Jesus Christ and the love of God and the fellowship of the Holy Spirit be with you all." This is a matter not of doctrine but of experience. In the same way, throughout the book of Ephesians there are many verses referring to the Divine Trinity, but they are for our experience. As we have seen, 1:3 speaks of the Father who has blessed us in the Son with every spiritual blessing; this also is not for doctrine but for our experience. According to doctrine alone, we can never understand the Divine Trinity, but by our experience we can realize that the Three are one God in actuality.

Several verses in the New Testament tell us clearly that the Holy Spirit today is in us. No one can argue with this. John 14:17, for example, says that the Spirit of reality would be in the disciples. There are also several verses that tell us that Christ is in us, such as Romans 8:10. In Galatians Paul said, "It pleased God...to reveal His Son in me" (1:15-16), "It is Christ who lives in me" (2:20), and "Christ is formed in you" (4:19). These verses do not speak of the Spirit of Christ or Christ in the Spirit; they clearly indicate that Christ Himself is in us. If Christ and the Spirit are not one, then there must be two who are in us, but to say this is heresy. How can we say that we have two in us? That there is one who is in us indicates that Christ is the Spirit. This illustrates that the Divine Trinity cannot be understood doctrinally. He must be realized by our experience. In our experience the Three of the Godhead are actually one. This is not merely my word; it is the word of the Bible.

Not only are Christ and the Spirit in us, but the Father also is in us. Ephesians 4:6 says, "One God and Father of all, who is over all and through all and in all." On the one hand, the Father, Son, and Spirit are three. Then are there three in us, or is there one in us? That there is one in us indicates that the Father is the Son and the Son is the Spirit; otherwise, there must be three in us. Again this illustrates that we can realize the Divine Trinity only by our experience. We can never define the Divine Trinity in the way of knowledge because our knowledge is too limited. In reality, in our experience, the Three are one.

In the Scriptures it is clear and unarguable that the Spirit is in us, Christ is in us, and the Father is in us. All Three today are in our spirit. We do not believe that the Three are separate and not one. Therefore, in Ephesians 3 the Three of the Godhead work together to fill us unto all the fullness of God. This means that the fullness of the Godhead is mingled with us. We are filled with the Triune God, and the Triune God mingles Himself with us. This is divinity mingled with humanity. We sometimes speak of the seven wonders of the world, but these are not the real wonders. In the entire universe the unique wonder is the Triune God in us. What a wonder that the Triune God is working Himself into us! We need to read Ephesians again, forgetting about traditional theology. Traditional theology damages us and hinders us from understanding the things in Ephesians. We must put all the above points together like a jigsaw puzzle. Then we will see the whole picture that the Father is in the Son, the Son is realized as the Spirit, and the Spirit is within us.

The Church as the Body of Christ in the Triune God

It is in this Triune God that we are all regenerated, transformed, composed, and built up as a Body for Christ with humanity mingled with divinity. This is a real wonder! In order to understand the church, we have to know the church in the way of one God, one Lord, one Spirit, and one Body (4:4-6). How can fallen people be the Body? It is by faith and baptism (v. 5). By faith we believe into the Triune God, and by baptism we are separated from the old things. However, we are still in the old creation with an old body, so we also need one hope of our calling (v. 4).

The one God is in the one Lord, the one Lord is the one Spirit, and the one Spirit is in the one Body. Now we share in this one Body by faith and baptism. This is the reason that everyone must believe in the Lord Jesus and be baptized. To believe in the Lord Jesus is to be identified with Christ and united with Him. To be baptized is to be buried, to have a clearance, a complete severance from the old living, the old creation, and all old matters. It is by faith and baptism that we have been transferred out of Adam into Christ. In this way we become the Body of the Triune God. However, we need something more because we still live in the old creation. In our spirit we are in the new creation, but our old body still remains in the old creation. Therefore, we hope in one thing— that Christ will return to saturate our body. By His life He will swallow up death, and by the newness of life He will swallow up all the oldness of the old creation. This is our hope. All the above verses show us the church in the Triune God, which is the aim of God's eternal purpose.

THE CHURCH AS THE NEW MAN, THE BODY, THE FULLNESS, THE BRIDE, THE DWELLING PLACE OF GOD, AND THE WARRIOR

Now we may see what the church is in God's intention. This is the third main point in Ephesians. In Ephesians there are at least seven different titles assigned to the church. First, it is the church and the new man. Ephesians 2:15 tells us that Christ created one new man in Himself out of two peoples, the Jews and the Gentiles. Our natural concept may be that the new man is an individual. Accordingly, we may think that there are many new men. However, the new man is not an individual man but a corporate man, because verse 15 says that it was created from two peoples.

Strictly speaking, when 4:22-24 says to put off the old man and put on the new man, it refers to the Body. We know this from 2:15b-16a, which says, "He might create the two in Himself into one new man, so making peace, and might reconcile both in one Body." This indicates that the one new man is the one Body, and the one Body is the one new man. The church is the new man, and this new man is the Body of Christ.

According to 1:23, this Body is also the fullness of the One who fills all in all. In addition, the church is the bride, the counterpart, of Christ, just as Eve was the counterpart to Adam (Eph. 5:23-32; Gen. 2:21-25). These four aspects of the church—the new man, the Body, the fullness, and the bride—form a group. The new man is the Body, the Body is the fullness, and the fullness is the counterpart. Besides these four aspects, the church is also God's habitation, His dwelling place in spirit (Eph. 2:21-22), and the soldier, the warrior (6:10-20). The warrior is not an army but a corporate Body to put on the whole armor of God. The whole armor of God is one item and not many. The one Body is one person that wears the whole armor.

The New Man with Christ as Life and the Body as His Fullness

Now we may see some of the details of the different aspects of the church. When a man is born, he has a human life. If we did not have the human life, we could not be a man.

That the church is the new man means that the church has a new life, and this new life is Christ. Christ is life to us because He is the very embodiment of the Father and is realized as the Spirit. This life, therefore, is the Triune God, who is typified by the tree of life. Originally, we were the old man because we had only the old life, the created life of man, but through Christ's crucifixion and resurrection He has regenerated us. Regeneration is simply the imparting of the Triune God into us. Through the processes of incarnation, crucifixion, and resurrection the Triune God has imparted Himself into us as life. Now we have a new life, the divine life. This life is God Himself in Christ as the Spirit. In this way we become the new man.

Moreover, this new man is the Body. The new man is a matter of life, while the Body is a matter of expression. Without a body a person can have no expression; no one could know him or recognize him. We are known and recognized by our body as our expression. That the church is the Body of Christ means that it is the very expression of Christ, and Christ is the life within the church.

The Body is the fullness of Christ. A head without a body is poor; it is without a fullness. Similarly, a disjointed body is not the fullness of the head. Only a proper body is the complete fullness of the head. In the four Gospels the Lord Jesus is the Head without the Body. Therefore, in the Gospels there is no fullness of Christ. In the book of Acts, however, Jesus is duplicated thousands of times. Hence, in Acts we can see the fullness of Christ. The church is composed of many members, and every member is a duplication, a living copy, of Jesus. These living members composed together form the Body.

The Body is the very expression of Christ, just as a person's physical body is his expression. This Body is also the fullness. Ephesians 1:23 does not speak of the fullness of Christ, the fullness of the Son of God, or the fullness of the Lord Jesus; it speaks of the fullness of the One who fills all in all. It is difficult to understand what the fullness is; this is too profound and our understanding is too limited. We also cannot explain how Christ fills all things. We can only say that this term shows how great Christ is. Today His fullness is a universal fullness because as the One who fills all in all He is unlimitedly great. He fills not only all but all in all. Christ is unlimited, and such an unlimited Christ needs a universal Body to be His fullness. Although the church on the earth may sometimes appear to be a mess, it is still in the principle of the fullness of Christ. Christ is in the United States, Europe, Africa, Asia, and in every place on the earth. The church as the Body is the universal fullness of Christ in both space and time.

The Counterpart of Christ

This fullness is also the counterpart of Christ, just as Eve was a counterpart to Adam to match Adam. That a wife is one with her husband typifies that the church is one with Christ; this is the great mystery in Ephesians 5:32. A husband and wife are like two halves of a watermelon. When the two halves are put together, they become a whole. One half needs the other half to match it. In the same way, the church is a part of Christ, the counterpart of Christ, to match Him. A wife is the fullness of the husband; in Genesis 2 Eve is both the counterpart and fullness of Adam. When Adam was a bachelor, he had no fullness, but when he was given a wife to match him as his counterpart, she became his fullness. Hence, the church in life and nature is one with Christ. The two have one life and one nature, so the church becomes a part of Christ to match Christ.

The Dwelling Place of God

The church is also the dwelling place of God. A person's body is his dwelling place. Strictly speaking, we do not live in a house; we live in our body. This is why the Scriptures liken our physical body to a dwelling place. In 2 Corinthians 5:1 Paul calls our fallen body an earthly tabernacle dwelling, a temporary dwelling, in contrast to a dwelling not made with hands, which will be our resurrected body in the future. Just as our body is the place in which we exist, our habitation, so the church is the Body of Christ to contain Christ and to express Him. Hence, it is the dwelling place, the habitation, of the Triune God.

As we have seen, the church as the new man is a matter of life, the church as the Body of Christ is a matter of expression, and the church as the bride of Christ is a counterpart. To speak of the church as the dwelling place of God, however, conveys the central thought of building. We need to be built up; this thought is very much revealed in Ephesians, as in 2:20-22 and 4:12 and 16. The church is the temple of God because it is God's habitation, God's dwelling place.

OUR NEED FOR EXPERIENCE

God dwells in the temple, but more specifically He dwells in the inner chamber of the temple. His Shekinah presence is in the Holy of Holies. The Holy of Holies is a type of our human spirit. Man is a temple of three parts, and our spirit is the innermost part. If we know how to discern and exercise our spirit, we can realize God's presence, which is His indwelling in the church. If we do not know how to use our spirit, to say that God is in the church is mere doctrine. We must learn how to discern and exercise our spirit in order to experience God's presence more and more in our spirit and in the church. We do not need doctrines but the conscious exercise of our spirit.

In Ephesians there are two prayers. The first prayer is a prayer for revelation (1:15-23), while the second prayer is a prayer for experience (3:14-19). At the beginning of this book we need a prayer for us to have revelation. Then, after we receive revelation, we need another prayer for us to experience what we see. Paul's first prayer is for us to have a spirit of wisdom and revelation in the full knowledge of Christ, while his second prayer is that our inner man would be strengthened with power that we may experience Christ in a full way, that Christ may make His home in us, that we may be filled unto all the fullness of the Triune God. This is the real experience of God being present in the church, particularly in our inner man.

Verse 16 says that we are strengthened not *in* the inner man but *into* the inner man. This means that the Holy Spirit deals with our inner man by working more and more of Christ into it. This requires us to practically discern, know, and exercise our spirit. However, the matter of our spirit is overlooked and even opposed by many Christians today. When we minister to people about Christ in our spirit, many of them are surprised; they have never heard this. Although they may receive much help from Christian workers to know the Word, memorize the Word, and understand the Word, they may never have been told how to exercise their spirit to experience Christ as the Spirit. To exercise our spirit is a very vital matter.

CHAPTER SEVENTEEN

CRUCIAL POINTS
CONCERNING THE CHURCH IN EPHESIANS

Scripture Reading: Eph. 2:1-6; 4:24; 5:22—6:9; 6:10-20; 1:3, 17; 2:22; 3:16; 4:23; 5:18

THE MATERIALS FOR THE CHURCH

In the previous chapter we saw the first three main points in Ephesians. The fourth main point is that this book shows us the real condition and nature of the materials for the building of the church. In the entire Scriptures there is no other book which reveals this as inclusively and deeply as this book. In their origin, the materials for the church were sinners, dead in sins. This is revealed clearly in Ephesians 2:1. Our nature was sinful, and we were dead in sins. The phrase *dead in sins* may be illustrated by a person who drowns; that person is dead in water. The water and this dead person become one. The person is in the water, the water is in that person, and the water buries that person. We may even say that this person is mingled with the water. The original condition and nature of each one of us is that we were in sin and death. Sin, just like the death waters, joined to us, buried us, and mingled with us.

Second, we were not only sinners but also enemies. We were rebels joined to and filled with the enemy of God, Satan (vv. 2-3). Satan, the ruler of the authority of the air, operated in the sons of disobedience, making us not only sinners according to God's righteousness but also rebels according to God's government and administration. We were rebels joined together with Satan, and we were filled with him. In other words, we were one with the enemy of God. This was our twofold condition and nature before we became the members of the Body. Even in Romans the apostle Paul did not reveal our original situation and condition so all-inclusively and deeply as in Ephesians. In Romans we are not told that we were dead in sins; we are only told that we were sinful. Neither does Romans tell us that we were rebels. Ephesians tells us that we were not only sinful but dead in sins, and not only sinners but rebels joined as one with God's enemy.

How marvelous it is that from such materials as these God produced the church! We praise God that in His great love He created from such materials, from sinners dead in sins and rebels joined to and filled with Satan, a glorious, marvelous, and wonderful Body for Christ.

THREE STEPS TAKEN BY GOD
TO PRODUCE THE CHURCH

Ephesians speaks of God's eternal purpose, the goal of His eternal purpose, what the church is, and what the original condition and nature of the materials for the church were. The fifth main point is the steps by which God produced the church. Verses 5 and 6 of chapter two say that even when we were dead in offenses, God made us alive together with Christ, raised us up together with Him, and seated us together with Him.

Making Us Alive Together with Christ

Because we were dead, God came in to make us alive, to impart life into us. God imparted Himself in Christ as the Spirit into us. In this way God made the dead materials alive. Ezekiel 37:1-14 contains a picture of this. God's people were likened to dry bones, dead and scattered. These dry bones signify the materials for the building of the Body. From these dry bones God built up His house, His dwelling place, and He formed an army to fight the battle for God. Originally these materials were dead and in the grave, but God breathed His breath into them; that is, He imparted His life into them, and the dry bones were made alive. To be made alive is to be regenerated.

Raising Us Up Together with Christ

Second, God raised us up not only from the grave but from the earth to the heavens. When we were dead in sins, we were fallen to the lowest level, even to the grave. But God raised us up to the highest point, even to the heavenlies.

Seating Us in the Heavenlies with Christ

Third, we were seated in the heavenlies with Christ. A person sits down only when his work is finished. Therefore, to be seated means that everything has been accomplished. In one sense, the church will be built, but in another sense, the church has been built up already. On the one hand, the Lord still must work on us, but on the other hand, He already has finished His work. He has made us alive, raised us to the heavenlies, and seated us together with Christ and in Christ.

When did God make us alive? When Christ was resurrected, His entire Body was made alive and raised up together with Him. Then in His ascension He brought us to the heavens and seated us with Him. Therefore, in God's divine point of view, the church has been built already; everything is complete. We may worry about the building of the church, but God does not worry because it already has been accomplished. We cannot understand this, but it is a fact which has been revealed to us.

John 2 records that when the Jews were trying to kill the Lord Jesus, He told them, "Destroy this temple, and in three days I will raise it up" (v. 19). When I was young I thought that this referred only to the resurrection of the Lord Jesus Himself. However, in these last years the Lord showed me that according to 1 Peter 1:3 all of us were regenerated through the resurrection of Christ. When Christ was crucified on the cross, we were crucified there also. In the same way, when Christ resurrected, we resurrected with Him. Therefore, we died in Him, were resurrected in Him, and were seated in Him. In God's sight everything has been accomplished and completed. Through Christ's resurrection and ascension the church has been produced. This is what is revealed to us in Ephesians 2.

Christ's History Becoming Our Experience

By the Transmission of the Spirit

What God accomplished through Christ and in Christ must become our experience. However, Christ is Christ, and we are we. He resurrected and ascended nearly two thousand years ago in a place far away. How then can the resurrection and ascension of Christ be our experience? How can we be in Christ, how can Christ be in us, and how can God's accomplishments in Christ be ours? It is not sufficient to answer that it is by identification. Even more, it is by the Spirit.

We may illustrate the Spirit by transmission through electricity. By means of electricity, something that happens in Los Angeles can immediately be brought into our presence. By the same transmission, people in America and the Far East can speak with one another. Without electricity, only my direct audience can hear me, but by the transmission of electricity, people in the uttermost part of the earth can hear me. Because of electricity, the problem of space and time is eliminated. In the same way, there is no problem of space or time with the Spirit. What Christ has accomplished and what God has wrought in Christ have all been compounded into the Spirit. Now the Spirit has come into us, and we have been put into the Spirit. Therefore, what Christ has accomplished is ours.

The church is produced by the resurrection and ascension of Christ, which are applied to us by the Spirit. If we take these matters merely as doctrine, they can never be our experience. They will merely be a formula in our mentality. Only when we realize these things in the spirit do they become our experience.

By Repenting and Believing

How can the Spirit come to us? It is by faith, and genuine, living faith always includes repentance. Faith without repentance is full of problems. A living faith always includes repentance. The Bible says, "Repent and believe" (Mark 1:15). Repentance and faith fit the requirements for the work of the Holy Spirit. The unique way for the Holy Spirit to work in us is through repentance and faith. There is no other way.

Whenever and wherever a person repents before God and believes in the Lord Jesus, immediately the Holy Spirit comes into him. This is a principle, a law. The way for radio waves in the air to enter a radio is to tune it properly. When we tune it to the right station, the radio waves operate according to a principle. In the same way, the principle of the work of the Spirit is for us to "tune to the station" of repentance and faith.

Every morning, every day, and every evening we need to repent and believe. We should pray, "Lord, forgive me. I admit that I am still sinful in so many things. I abhor myself, and I repent before You. Lord, I open myself to You, and I put my trust in You. I believe You!" By doing this, we tune ourselves properly and pick up the heavenly "radio waves"; that is, in our experience we receive the Holy Spirit. Now the Spirit is in us, and we are in the Spirit. In this way, whatever has been accomplished in Christ and by Christ is ours. Christ's history becomes our experience in the Spirit.

The wonderful, all-inclusive Spirit comes into us through our repentance and faith. Without exception, whether a person is low or high, young or old, weak or strong, foolish or clever, uneducated or educated, evil or good, as long as he repents and believes in the Lord Jesus, the Spirit as the spiritual, heavenly "radio waves" comes into him. This wonderful Spirit transmits all that Christ is, all that Christ has done, and all that God has accomplished in Christ into us. Then we are in the Spirit, and the Spirit is in us. We are made alive, raised up, and seated with Christ in the Spirit. Without the Spirit as the transmission we cannot be one with Christ; He will be separated from us by space and time. But in the Holy Spirit as the transmission we are one with Christ regardless of space or time. In this way, the church is produced by the resurrection and ascension of Christ applied to us by the Spirit.

THE DAILY WALK OF THE MEMBERS
OF THE BODY OF CHRIST

In the Spirit and in the Body

The sixth main point in Ephesians is the daily walk of the members of Christ's Body on this earth. After we become members of the Body of Christ, we should have a daily walk in the Spirit and in the Body. This is a basic teaching of this book.

The first three chapters of Ephesians are a revelation of the life, nature, and position of the church, while the last three chapters deal with the walk of the church. The first item of the walk of the church is to keep the oneness of the Body. This is to realize the Body life. To realize the Body life is first of all to keep the oneness of the Body. Whether we are an apostle or a small brother or sister, we are the members of the Body and for the Body. Therefore, we must keep the oneness of the Body and live in the Body.

For many years after I was saved, no one told me about the oneness of the Body. I received many teachings concerning Christian ethics and human ethics with Christian terminology. At that time I was bothered. I asked myself what the difference is between the ethics taught by Confucius and the things taught in the Scriptures. In my upbringing I had studied Confucius, and I was familiar with his teaching of ethics. I considered that those ethics were so good that there was no need for me to be taught by the Scriptures. At that time I did not know the difference. Gradually, the Lord showed me that the teachings of the Scriptures are absolutely different. The Christian walk on this earth is not a matter of ethics. It is a matter of living as a member of the Body of Christ.

We must realize that we are members and that we need to live in the Body. We should never be independent; we should never be separated from the Body. We should always live, walk, and work in the church, the Body of Christ. We must walk in the Spirit and in the Body, and we must put on the new man (4:24). To put on the new man is simply to live in the Body. This includes our functioning as members in the Body.

In God's Order and Government

The Christian walk is also a walk in God's order (5:22—6:9). In our human relationships there must be God's order. Whether you are a wife or a husband, you must keep your position. Whether you are a child or a parent, you also must keep your position. Even masters and slaves have their own positions. All of these relationships were not invented by man. Rather, they were arranged by God. They are matters involving God's government and God's administration. The Christian walk is one that keeps God's order in human relationships. This is very important. It is not merely a matter of ethics; it is a matter of obedience to God's government. If we do not stand in our proper position to keep God's order, we are rebellious against God's government. If God created you as a woman and married you to a husband, you have to keep your position and stand in it. This maintains the right order. Then you will be obedient, not rebellious, to God's government.

For wives to be submissive to their husbands is not a matter of mere ethics. We must have the highest viewpoint concerning these things. Human relationships are matters related to God's government. The teachings of Confucius are from the human point of view, but the teachings in the book of Ephesians are from the heavenly point of view, showing us the order in God's government. For a child not to honor his parents is against not only human ethics but even more against God's government. The young brothers and sisters must see that to go against ethics may be a small matter, but to go against the divine government is very serious. If a child honors his parents, he will receive the blessing. If he keeps the order in God's government, he will enjoy all that God has arranged. Otherwise, he will be grieved.

God's order in His government expresses God Himself. Why are there husbands? It is to express Christ. Why are there parents? Parents are the expression of God as the Father. Similarly, why are there masters? Masters are the representatives of God as the Lord and the Master. In all of these relationships God is expressed and represented. God arranged these human relationships in order to express Himself. Therefore, if we are disobedient against God's order, we damage God's expression and representation. In a marriage relationship, the husband and wife are a representation of Christ and the church. If a wife does not keep her proper order and rises up to become the head, the representation of Christ and the church in their home is spoiled. This is not merely a matter of ethics and morality. It is a matter of God's government and God's representation.

The arrangement of the entire universe is a representation of God Himself. When all things keep their proper position in the right order, God is represented and expressed. But if any part of creation does not keep its position and breaks the order, the representation and expression of God is damaged in that part. We must see the book of Ephesians from this point of view.

We were created and arranged according to the order in God's government to represent God and express God. The race of Adam failed the Lord in this matter, but the Lord by His redemption has brought us back and strengthened us with Himself as life within us. Now we must keep our position in the proper order to represent God and express God in our daily walk. Therefore, the walk of the church is by the Spirit, in the Body, and for the representation and expression of God.

In Christ

The walk of the church is a walk not only in the Spirit but also in Christ. Christ is the essence, reality, centrality, and universality of this walk. Our walk must be a walk that expresses Christ, exalts Christ, testifies Christ, ministers Christ, releases Christ, and shares Christ with others. In summary, our walk today must be a walk by the Spirit, in the Body, in the order and government of God, and in Christ. This is the walk of the church today on this earth.

THE CHURCH AS THE WARRIOR
FOR DEFEATING GOD'S ENEMY

The seventh main point revealed in Ephesians is the enemy of God, Satan, the devil, who frustrates and damages God's purpose (2:2; 6:11-12). Although Ephesians is a short book of six chapters, it is very inclusive, even touching the spiritual warfare. This book and its sister book, Colossians, tell us that the enemy of God is the ruler of the evil forces in the air. The term *ruler* indicates that he has a kingdom, and under him are the principalities, authorities, powers, legions, and dominions. In his kingdom there are officers that help him to reign; these are the evil spirits, the spirits of darkness and wickedness. This evil one is always doing his best to frustrate and damage God's eternal purpose. The eternal purpose of God is to have the church, but the enemy of God frustrates God's purpose. Therefore, there is a conflict. God fights this battle through the church, and the church fights the battle for God.

Ephesians shows us how the church expresses God's interests on the positive side and deals with God's enemy on the negative side. The two important aspects of God's creation of man are that man was created in the image of God to express Him and that man was committed by God with His authority to represent Him in order to deal with His enemy. Man was created to rule the earth and in particular to rule over the creeping things, among which is the serpent, the devil (Gen. 1:26). In Ephesians there are also these two main items. First, the church is the expression of the Triune God; 4:24 tells us that the new man was created according to God, that is, in His image. Then the last chapter tells us that the church fights against God's enemy to deal with the evil forces (6:10-20).

This battle is fought by the church in Christ Himself as the might and the power. Therefore, we must stand in the Lord, be strong in Him, and fight the battle by Christ as the whole armor of God. The different items of the armor are the different aspects of Christ that we experience. The more we experience Christ, the more we have the armor to cover and protect us to fight the spiritual warfare in Christ as the power and by Christ as the armor. Moreover, the unique way to fight the battle in Christ as our strength, power, and armor is in spirit and by prayer (v. 18).

THE TWO SPIRITS

If we take care of all the foregoing main points, we will be able to understand the entire book of Ephesians. This entire book very much concentrates on the Spirit. Chapter one tells us that God has blessed us with every spiritual blessing (v. 3) and that we have been sealed with the Holy Spirit (v. 13). God has put the divine Holy Spirit into us, and we are filled by the Spirit. Chapter one also tells us that we need a spirit of wisdom and revelation (v. 17). Chapter two continues to tell us that the church is the dwelling place of God in spirit (v. 22). If we are not in spirit, we cannot be God's dwelling place. Only when an appliance is connected to the electrical current can it be the dwelling place of the electricity. As the dwelling place of God, we must be in spirit. Chapter three tells us that we need to be strengthened with power through the Spirit into our inner man, our spirit (v. 16). The most important verse in chapter four is verse 23, which says, "Be renewed in the spirit of your mind." Following this, 5:18 tells us to be filled in spirit, and 6:18 charges us to pray at every time in spirit.

All the matters and teachings in Ephesians are realized in spirit, that is, in the Holy Spirit mingled with our human spirit. These two spirits are mingled as one. Hence, in order to realize and experience all that is mentioned in this book, we must know how to exercise our spirit. We must know how to use our spirit and how to realize the Holy Spirit working in our spirit. All spiritual experiences are concentrated into this mingled spirit—the Holy Spirit mingled with the human spirit. The book of Ephesians is now open to us, but it can only be realized in spirit. If we do not know how to exercise our spirit to realize the Holy Spirit, all of these matters will be mere doctrines in our memory. In order to transfer all these items into our experience, we need the exercise of our spirit.

CHAPTER EIGHTEEN

THE EXPERIENCE OF CHRIST IN PHILIPPIANS

Scripture Reading: Phil. 1:19-21; 2:5-8, 15, 17; 3:7-11, 14; 4:12-13

The subject of the book of Philippians is the experience of Christ in every kind of circumstance. No other book deals as specifically with the experience of Christ as this one, telling us that Christ must be our experience regardless of our circumstances and difficulties.

Students of the Scriptures may ask why the book of Philippians is inserted between the two sister books of Ephesians and Colossians. I believe that there is a sovereign meaning to this; I wholly believe in the sovereign arrangement of these books in the New Testament. The book of Ephesians is concerning the church, and the church is a matter of a life in Christ. If we intend to have the church life, we need the experience of Christ. We can never separate the church life from the experience of Christ as life. We can never realize the church in a living way if we do not experience Christ in our daily walk. We have to experience Christ in all our circumstances; only then can we realize the church life.

The church is not a matter of mere doctrine. We cannot realize the church merely by teaching or by studying. Rather, it requires the real experience of the life of Christ. The more we experience Christ's life, the more we will sense the need for the church. When we live by ourselves apart from Christ, we do not sense the need for the church. But when we come to Christ and begin to experience Him, right away we sense the need for the church life. Thus, the experience of Christ as life is basic to the realization of the church life. Because of this, Philippians, the book on the experience of Christ, immediately follows Ephesians, the book on the church. This is the meaning of the sovereign order of these books. The more we love Christ and live in Him, by Him, and with Him, and the more we experience Him, the more we sense our deep need for the church.

LIVING CHRIST TO MAGNIFY HIM

Philippians has four chapters, and each chapter is a section. Chapter one shows us that Christ is our life and expression. In other words, this chapter tells us how we live Christ to magnify Him, that is, to express Him.

Living by Christ as Our Life
and for Christ as Our Purpose

Verse 21 of chapter one says, "For to me, to live is Christ." This has the meaning both of living by Christ as our life and of living for Christ as our purpose. While we are on this earth, we live not by ourselves but by Christ as our life, and we live not for ourselves but for Christ as our purpose. If we live for ourselves, we cannot say that for us to live is Christ; we would have to say that for us to live is we ourselves. If it is true that for us to live is Christ, this means that we are living by Christ and for Christ. Christ is our life and Christ is our purpose.

Verse 20 says, "According to my earnest expectation and hope that in nothing I will be put to shame, but with all boldness, as always, even now Christ will be magnified in my body, whether through life or through death." To say that Christ is magnified in us is abstract, but to say that Christ is magnified in our body is more concrete. Whether through life or through death, Christ will be magnified in us bodily. *Magnified* means expressed, exalted, and honored. Christ is expressed, exalted, and honored in us bodily. This means that we are living here to express Christ, exalt Christ, and honor Christ, and our life, living, and being are to follow Christ as our purpose. The purpose of our living, of our family, of our job, and of everything in our life is Christ Himself. Our purpose is to magnify Christ, express Christ, glorify Christ, exalt Christ, and honor Christ.

Although it is an easy thing to quote this verse, do we really live for Christ? Is everything of ours on the altar for Christ? We should remember who it is that wrote this word. The apostle Paul put everything on the altar, and he left nothing for himself. Everything of his was an offering, either put on the altar or poured out at the base of the altar. While he was in prison, everything had been taken away for Christ; all that was left to him was his breath. Such a person was qualified to say, "For to me, to live is Christ." We may not be qualified to say this, because we may not be one hundred percent for Christ. We must be wholly for Christ. While we do business, our business is for Christ. Our job, our studying, our teaching, and everything in our life is for Christ. Whatever happens to us, whatever we have, and whatever we do must all be for Christ. Then we will be in a position to say that for us, to live is Christ. We should check ourselves in this light. Verses 20 and 21 are the key verses in the first section of this book, showing how the apostle Paul took Christ as his life and as his expression.

The Bountiful Supply of the Spirit of Jesus Christ

Verse 19 of chapter one is another verse which is very precious yet very much neglected by Christians today. This verse speaks of the bountiful supply of the Spirit of Jesus Christ. Conybeare tells us that the Greek word for *supply* is a technical word, referring to the choragus, the leader of the chorus on the Greek stage. The choragus was responsible to supply all the needs of the members of the chorus. Their clothing, food, musical instruments, and everything they needed was provided by the choragus. Paul used this same word to describe the supply of the Spirit of Jesus Christ. Therefore, this word may be rendered as *bountiful supply,* a supply that meets all our needs.

The term *the Spirit of Jesus Christ* is richer than *the Spirit of God.* The Spirit of God at the beginning of the Old Testament was not as rich as the Spirit of Jesus Christ after Pentecost. In the Old Testament times, within the Spirit of Jehovah there were not the elements of the humanity of the Lord Jesus, His suffering in His human life, the effectiveness of His death, and the power of His resurrection. However, on the day of Pentecost the Spirit was poured out from the ascended Christ, and within this Spirit were all these elements.

A cup of plain water contains only the water, but if we add tea, sugar, and other ingredients, the water becomes richer. This is a picture of the bountiful supply of the Spirit of Jesus Christ. To speak only of the Spirit of God is not sufficient; today the Spirit of God is the Spirit of Jesus Christ. In this Spirit there is divinity, the heavenly element, and there is also humanity, the suffering of the Lord Jesus in His human life on earth, His crucifixion, and His resurrection.

The Spirit of Jesus Christ may be compared to an all-inclusive dose of medicine. When we take this dose, one element kills germs, another element supplies nourishment, and other elements supply other needs. The reason that Paul could live Christ and magnify Him, the reason he was able to say, "For to me, to live is Christ," is that he had the bountiful supply of the Spirit of Jesus Christ. As a member of the "chorus," Paul was bountifully supplied by the Choragus. This is the proper meaning of Philippians 1:19.

We also are members of the "chorus," and the Holy Spirit is the choragus to satisfy all our needs. We are human beings, and within the Spirit is the human nature. We are suffering on the earth, and within Him there is the element of the suffering of human life. We need the cross as our killing element, and within the Spirit there is this element. We also need His resurrection power, and within the Spirit of Jesus Christ there is this power. Whatever we need today is in the Spirit of Jesus Christ. By the bountiful supply of the Spirit of Jesus Christ we can live Christ to magnify Him, and we can say, "For to me, to live is Christ."

TAKING CHRIST AS THE PATTERN

By Lowering Our Position and Standard

Philippians 2 is the second section, showing us Christ as our pattern, our living example. The principle of this pattern is that someone with the highest life and position would be willing to live in a humble way. Christ has the highest life, the life of God, and He has the highest position, which is equality with God, yet He would not grasp that. Rather, He temporarily set it aside (vv. 5-8). To have grasped His equality with God would not have been wrong. Although He had the human nature, it would have been right for Him to take the standing of God. However, He would not grasp that. He put aside His position of equality with God, and He lived in the most humble and lowly way. This is the principle of Christ as the pattern.

We all have to learn this. If today by the sovereignty of God we have a high position and much wealth, we have to lower ourselves. We must lower our position and standard in our living according to the example of Christ. It is not wrong to grasp our position and say that it is something that God has given us to enjoy, but if we do this, we are not taking Christ as our person and pattern. The pattern given to us by Christ is that one has a life in the highest position, yet he is willing to live a life in the lowliest way. We all must learn to lower our position and standard. We may be millionaires, but we should be willing to lower our standard of living and use our substance for the glory of God and the benefit of others. This is the example of Christ, and this is the principle of Christ as a pattern to us who take Him as our life.

If we say that we take Christ as our life and yet do not take Him as our pattern, there is something wrong. In the past I have seen a number of good brothers and sisters in high positions, such as bank managers and university professors, who did love the Lord. Yet to my realization, some of them were not willing to humble themselves and take a lower position. On the one hand, they have the right to enjoy their position; to grasp one's position is not robbery. However, Christ for the glory of God and for our benefit emptied and humbled Himself to live not as God but as a slave. He truly had the position of God, being equal with God, yet He humbled Himself to live as a slave.

Some brothers and sisters are rich only for themselves. When they enjoy their own riches, they are generous to themselves, but in giving their riches to others they are not generous. Their way of living is to spend their wealth and their riches for their own enjoyment. They are not willing to give their wealth for God's glory and work. No one can condemn them, because according to their position it is legal and right to do this. However, if they mean business to take Christ as their life and pattern, they should lower their standard in the way they spend for their living.

The principle of Christ as the pattern for our living is that even if we have the highest standard, the highest position, we should not grasp it. We should put that aside and lower our standard. As long as we can live on the earth, that is good enough. We should save the rest of what we have for the glory of God and the benefit of others. If we would not do this, if we would keep our standard and grasp our position, we will waste what God has given us.

Verse 17 says, "But even if I am being poured out as a drink offering upon the sacrifice and service of your faith, I rejoice, and I rejoice together with you all." This person, who took Christ as his pattern, offered everything on the altar. This verse says that Paul himself was being poured out. To be poured out is to lower one's standard and position in his living.

To Shine as Luminaries in the World

Verse 15 says, "That you may be blameless and guileless, children of God without blemish in the midst of a crooked and perverted generation, among whom you shine as luminaries in the world." These are two key verses in this chapter. One says that Paul was being poured out as a drink offering, and the other says that we shine as luminaries. We cannot shine as luminaries until we lower the standard of our living and are willing to give up our rightful position. We should not grasp our position. To proclaim that we are professors or bank managers is to grasp our position, but if a professor would go to the street corners on Saturdays and distribute tracts to the people, he will be shining. If Christ while on earth grasped His position as God, no light would have shined forth. He gave up the high standard of being equal with God, put it aside, and lowered Himself to live in poverty as a lowly man from

Nazareth. Because of this, men saw the light shining through Him and out of Him.

Besides verses 15 and 17, verses 6 and 7 are also crucial, saying, "Who, existing in the form of God, did not consider being equal with God a treasure to be grasped, but emptied Himself, taking the form of a slave, becoming in the likeness of men." For Christ to empty Himself, to make Himself of no reputation, means that He lowered His standard. In our living and in the things we do, we must lower our standard. We should not try to be honored by people. To try to be honored by people is a wrong concept in our Christian walk. Rather, we may be despised by others.

For Christ to keep His position of equality with God would not have been robbery. It was one hundred percent legal and right, but He gave that up. He lowered Himself and made Himself of no reputation. He was despised as a lowly carpenter from Nazareth. This is our pattern. We should not talk about taking Christ as our life in a vain way. To speak in vain about taking Christ as life is to enjoy a kind of entertainment. If we are serious, we have to lower our position and standard and be willing to be poured out on the altar as a drink offering. Then the light will shine through us. This is the key to Philippians 2.

CHRIST AS OUR GOAL AND AIM

Chapter three of Philippians shows us that Christ must be our goal and our aim. Verse 14 speaks of the goal. We are in a race, and our goal is the all-inclusive Christ. When the apostle Paul wrote this Epistle in approximately A.D. 64, he was already quite old and had been running the Christian race for a long time. Although Paul was aged and very experienced in Christ, he did not have the assurance that he had arrived at the goal. He was even afraid that he would miss the mark. So he said, "Forgetting the things which are behind and stretching forward to the things which are before, I pursue toward the goal" (vv. 13b-14a). The goal is Christ Himself as the prize to be awarded to us. In the Old Testament the good land of Canaan was the goal for all the people of Israel after they were saved and delivered out of Egypt. While they were wandering and pressing on in the wilderness, they had a goal ahead of them. The good land of Canaan is a type of Christ, who is our goal.

Being Conformed to the Death of Christ by the Power of His Resurrection

There are many important verses in Philippians 3. Verse 10 begins, "To know Him." Paul knew Christ already, but he desired to know Him more. This verse continues, "And the power of His resurrection and the fellowship of His sufferings, being conformed to His death." The death of Christ is a form, like a mold used for cooking. God puts us as pieces of dough into the mold of Christ's death, onto His cross. When a person makes a cake, he conforms the dough to the form of the mold. In the same way, God puts us into the mold of Christ's death to conform us to it.

This is by the resurrection power. Within us is the resurrection power and without is the cross, the mold, in our circumstances. Paul's imprisonment provided the circumstances in which he was put into the mold of Christ's death that he might be conformed to His death. By himself there was no strength to do this. The strength was the resurrection power within him.

Attaining to the Out-resurrection

In chapter three of Philippians, the word *resurrection* is used twice. The first time it refers to the resurrection power by which we are conformed to the death of Christ (v. 10). Then verse 11 says, "If perhaps I may attain to the out-resurrection from the dead." Many translations of this verse are not adequate; the translators neglected the first part of the Greek word for *resurrection* because they did not have the proper light. The word *resurrection* is composed with a prefix and should be translated *extra-resurrection* or *out-resurrection*. The out-resurrection is something special. Many verses in the New Testament tell us that at the coming of the Lord Jesus, all the saved persons who have died in the Lord will be resurrected. However, there is a difference in the way they will participate in that resurrection. Of all those who share in that resurrection, some will enjoy a special resurrection, an outstanding resurrection. This may be compared to a graduating class. Although all the students graduate, only the top ones share an outstanding graduation, an "extra-graduation." Paul was pursuing this special resurrection.

The out-resurrection is nothing less than a special portion of Christ experienced by us. A special portion of Christ will be awarded to certain ones. This is similar to the hidden manna, which is different from the open manna (Rev. 2:17; Exo. 16:14-15). Both the open manna and the hidden manna are a type of Christ, but the hidden manna is a special portion. Christ is the resurrection in a general way (John 11:25), but Christ as the out-resurrection is a special portion of Christ as a reward.

Counting All Things as Loss in Order to Gain Christ

All young believers should learn to recite Philippians 3:7 and 8. Paul says, "But what things were gains to me, these I have counted as loss on account of Christ. But moreover I also count all things to be loss on account of the excellency of the knowledge of Christ Jesus my Lord, on account of whom I have suffered the loss of all things and count them as refuse that I may gain Christ." *What things* in verse 7 refers to the religious things, the things in Judaism as mentioned in the previous verses. Paul dropped all those religious things for Christ. In verse 8, however, Paul dropped not only the religious things but *all things* on account of the excellency of the knowledge of Christ Jesus. All the above verses show us that Christ is not only our life and pattern but also our goal and our aim. We drop all other things and pursue nothing but Christ. Our goal is to gain Christ.

CHRIST AS OUR SECRET AND POWER

Being Initiated with the Basic Principles to Solve Every Problem

Chapter four reveals to us that Christ is our secret and our power, our strength. Verses 12 and 13 say, "I know also how to be abased, and I know how to abound; in everything and in all things I have learned the secret both to be filled and to hunger, both to abound and to lack. I am able to do all things in Him who empowers me." In Greek the phrase *I have learned the secret* means "I have been initiated." This may be illustrated by mathematics. When we teach a young student addition, subtraction, multiplication, and division, we initiate him by giving him the basic principles. In this way he learns the secret. Whenever he comes across a problem in mathematics, he knows the secret of how to solve it.

Christ is not only our power but our secret. We live by this power, and we live by this secret. Then whatever matter comes to us, we can solve it. Because we know the secret, we do not care whether we are rich or poor or whether we are abased or we abound. The unbelievers in the world are foolish because they do not know the secret. They are like people who have never learned the principles of mathematics; no matter what problem they come across, they cannot solve it. We are not this kind of person. We have been initiated in Christ, with Christ, and by Christ. Because Christ is our secret, we know how to face any kind of situation. Whether people honor us or despise us, we know the secret and we have the power. Christ is our secret, and Christ is also our power.

By the Transmission of Christ as the Spirit

If Christ were not the Spirit, He could not be our power within. Therefore, we must come back to the Spirit. We can never and should never forget Philippians 1:19, which speaks of the bountiful supply of the Spirit of Jesus Christ. If Christ were not the "electricity," how could He be the power to us? He is the electricity transmitted to us by the Spirit as the current. The current, the transmission, of the electricity is the electricity itself, just as the circulation of blood is the blood itself flowing. Without the blood, there is no circulation, but we use the term *circulation* to describe the movement of the blood. In the same way, the Holy Spirit is the transmission of the Lord, although in actuality the Spirit is the Lord Himself.

If the Lord Himself were not the Spirit as the transmission, how could He be subjective to us? How could we be in

Him and He in us? In John 15:4 the Lord Jesus said, "Abide in Me and I in you." The only way to abide in Christ and for Him to abide in us is by the Spirit. This is the reason John 14 indicates that Christ was to be transfigured as the Spirit. Christ could not abide in us and we could not abide in Him until the things mentioned John 14 were accomplished. Now Christ is the Spirit (John 14:16-18; 2 Cor. 3:17), and as the Spirit He enters into us. In this way, we are in Him and He is in us. He and we, we and He, become a mutual abode; we abide in Him and He abides in us. This is a matter entirely of the Spirit. Therefore, we repeat this vital point: We must know our spirit and realize the Holy Spirit. For Christ to be our power and our secret is not an objective matter; it is one hundred percent subjective to us. If we know Him in the spirit and as the Spirit, we will experience Him.

If we are impressed deeply with all of these points in the four sections of Philippians, this book will be very clear to us. We must take Christ as our life and our expression, our pattern and our example, our goal and our aim, and our secret and our power. Then we can do all things in Him who empowers us. He is our secret. Galatians, Ephesians, Philippians, and Colossians are four wonderful books in the Bible. If we experience the Christ in Galatians and Philippians, we will know His Body in Ephesians; then we will realize Christ as the Head in Colossians.

CHAPTER NINETEEN

CHRIST AS EVERYTHING IN COLOSSIANS

(1)

Scripture Reading: Col. 1:9; 4:12; 2:2; 1:15-18; 2:9, 16-17; 1:12; 3:4

Although this is a short book of only four chapters, there are many main points that we need to see. Almost every matter in this book is a main point.

KNOWING CHRIST AS THE WILL OF GOD

Colossians is a book concerning God's will. In the first chapter Paul says, "Therefore we also, since the day we heard of it, do not cease praying and asking on your behalf that you may be filled with the full knowledge of His will in all spiritual wisdom and understanding" (1:9). Wisdom is in our spirit for us to realize, sense, and perceive the spiritual things, while understanding is in our mind to interpret what we perceive. We need all spiritual wisdom and understanding in order to have the full knowledge of the will of God. The will of God mentioned here is not His will in small matters. It is not merely for us to know what school to go to, what house to buy, or whether or not to marry. These things are too minor. The will of God mentioned here is the eternal will of God, the great will of God. It is related not to the things in our daily life but to God's purpose, God's intention. To know this will requires that we have full knowledge and all spiritual wisdom and understanding.

What is the will of God according to His desire, His intention, in the whole universe, in creation, in redemption, in the coming age, and in eternity? The entire book of Colossians is

the answer to this question. If we read this book, we will realize that the answer is Christ Himself. The will of God is in
Christ, concentrated in Christ, and for Christ. Christ is everything in the will of God. We must know this and realize this
with spiritual wisdom and with our understanding in a clear,
renewed mind.

The last chapter of this book tells us, "Epaphras, who is
one of you, a slave of Christ Jesus, greets you, always struggling on your behalf in his prayers that you may stand
mature and fully assured in all the will of God" (4:12). In the
first chapter the apostle Paul and his co-workers prayed that
the Colossians would know the will of God, and in the last
chapter Epaphras as a slave of Christ struggled fervently in
prayer on behalf of the church concerning the same thing.
Therefore, this is a book which reveals to us the eternal will
of God in the universe. We must keep these two verses in
mind.

GOD BEING A MYSTERY

In writing Colossians the apostle was much in the spirit,
expressing from the spirit of prayer what was on his heart
and in his spirit. As a result, it is difficult to divide this book
into sections. The best way to know this book, therefore, is to
see not the sections but the main points. There are at least
seven main points revealed in this book.

First, Colossians speaks of the mystery of God in relation
to the will of God. In order to speak about a person's will, we
must know what is in his heart. We must know him, understand him, and know what type of person he is. God has a
mystery, and He is a mystery. We know that God exists, but
apparently it is difficult for anyone to know Him. Not only
God Himself is a mystery, but what He desires and intends to
do is also a mystery.

The term *the mystery of God* is found in Colossians 2:2.
This verse says, "Unto all the riches of the full assurance
of understanding, unto the full knowledge of the mystery
of God, Christ." Here the apostle uses such spiritual terms
as *all the riches, full assurance of understanding,* and
full knowledge. The mystery of God is too mysterious, too

profound, and too great. It needs all the riches of the full assurance of understanding. What is the mystery of God? By ourselves we cannot thoroughly explain what God is and what God intends to do; the answer is in the book of Colossians.

CHRIST BEING THE MYSTERY OF GOD

The King James Version renders the last part of 2:2 as "the mystery of God, and of the Father, and of Christ." This requires an evaluation of the different Greek manuscripts of the New Testament. Many manuscripts differ in their renderings. The King James Version was translated in 1611, and John Nelson Darby published his New Translation in the second half of the previous century. Some of the best and most trustworthy manuscripts were discovered in the last two centuries. By 1901 the translators of the American Standard Version had many good manuscripts in their hands, so we trust more in their decision of which term to use. The American Standard Version renders this verse, "The mystery of God, even Christ," but the word *even* is not in the Greek text; it is supplied by the translators. Therefore, the best rendering of verse 2 is "the mystery of God, Christ."

The Image of the Invisible God

The mystery of God is Christ Himself. This is a very significant word. God and His intention are great, profound, and mysterious, yet Christ is this mystery. This is far beyond our understanding. Nevertheless, according to the record of this book, we can point out three items related to Christ being the mystery of God. First, Christ is the very image of the invisible God (1:15). God Himself is invisible, so He is a mystery. We cannot see Him; neither can we understand this mystery. Moreover, what He intends to do is also a mystery. However, Colossians tell us that Christ is the image of the invisible God. An image is an expression; that Christ is the image of God means that He is the expression, the explanation, of what God is. As such, He is the Word of God. John 1:1 says, "In the beginning was the Word, and the Word was with God, and the Word was God," and verse 18 says, "No one has ever seen God; the only begotten Son, who is in the bosom of the Father, He has declared Him." As the Word of God, Christ declares, defines, and expresses God.

The Fullness of the Godhead

Second, Colossians 2:9 says, "For in Him dwells all the fullness of the Godhead bodily." God is embodied in Christ; all that God is and has within Himself, that is, all the fullness of the Godhead, dwells in Christ bodily. Therefore, Christ is not only the expression, the image, of God but also the reality of God, the very embodiment of God. To find the meaning of *fullness,* we should not use our imagination but rather trace the usage of this word in the divine record. This takes us to John 1, where verse 14 says, "And the Word became flesh and tabernacled among us...full of grace and reality," and verse 16 says, "For of His fullness we have all received, and grace upon grace." *His fullness* is the fullness of God. Since the fullness of the Godhead dwells in Christ, we have all received of His fullness.

When the Son of God was incarnated as a man, with Him there was the fullness of God, and of this fullness we have all received. In order to know the items that we have received, we must further trace through the Gospel of John. John tells us that we receive life, light, the way, truth, food, and drink. All of these are only a few of the items of the fullness of God. All the fullness of God dwells in Christ, who is the very embodiment of God. He is the life, the light, the way, the reality, the food, and the drink. He is everything because the fullness of God is embodied in Him. He is the very embodiment of all the elements of God. What God is and what God has are embodied in Christ.

The Center of God's Will

Christ is also the center of God's will. All that God planned is related to Christ. Christ as the mystery of God includes these three matters—the image of God, the embodiment of God, and the very center of God's will.

CHRIST AS EVERYTHING

As the Creator, the Firstborn of Creation, the Firstborn from the Dead, and the Head of the Body

The third major point in Colossians is that God intends to make Christ everything. In the universe the first item is God. Then there is God's creation, including man. In addition, there is redemption, which includes the church. These five items—God, God's creation with man as the center, and God's redemption with the church as the center—include all the items in the universe. The first chapter of Colossians reveals that Christ is God (vv. 15a, 19), Christ is part of the creation (v. 15b), and Christ accomplished redemption (vv. 20-22). Verses 15 through 18 say, "Who is the image of the invisible God, the Firstborn of all creation, because in Him all things were created, in the heavens and on the earth, the visible and the invisible, whether thrones or lordships or rulers or authorities; all things have been created through Him and unto Him. And He is before all things, and all things cohere in Him; and He is the Head of the Body, the church; He is the beginning, the Firstborn from the dead, that He Himself might have the first place in all things." Christ Himself is both the Creator and the Firstborn of all creation. The creation came out of Him and was made by Him. Without Him there is no creation, but at the same time He is the first item of all created things. *The Firstborn of all creation* refers to God's old creation, while *the Firstborn from the dead* refers to God's redemption. Both in God's creation and in God's redemption Christ is the Firstborn.

In these few verses there are several items of what Christ is. Christ is the very Creator; the first item, the Firstborn, in creation; and the Firstborn in God's redemption; therefore, He is the Head of the church. Christ is everything. He also became a genuine man in God's creation. This corresponds with the record in the first chapter of John's Gospel, which says, "In the beginning was the Word, and the Word was with God, and the Word was God....All things came into being through Him, and apart from Him not one thing came into being which has come into being" (vv. 1, 3). Then verse 14 says that the Word became flesh, incarnated to become a man, in order to accomplish redemption. He is also the Head of the church, and He is the church, the Body itself (1 Cor. 12:12). Therefore, He is everything.

As the Reality of All Things

Verses 16 and 17 of Colossians 2 say, "Let no one therefore judge you in eating and in drinking or in respect of a feast or of a new moon or of the Sabbath, which are a shadow of the things to come, but the body is of Christ." These two verses indicate that the reality of all that we need is Christ. We need food, drink, and the feasts. A new moon indicates a new start, and the Sabbath is for rest. However, all these are simply a shadow; they are not the real things. Christ Himself is the reality of all these things.

When a person stands in the light, he casts a shadow, but the shadow is not the real person. The real person is the body of that shadow. All things in the entire universe are only a shadow; Christ Himself is the reality. The clothes that we wear are not the real clothes; they are shadows. Christ is our real clothing. If we do not have Christ to clothe us, we are still naked before God. The light we see is not the real light. Christ is the reality of the light. Even if we have the best light, without Christ we are still in darkness. The sun is not the real sun; it is a type. The reality of the sun is Christ, the Sun of righteousness (Mal. 4:2). Even the house in which we dwell is not our real dwelling place. Our real dwelling place is Christ. Everything we need is a shadow; the reality of all things is Christ. To be sure, Christ is not the reality of the negative things in the universe, such as sin, the world, self, Satan, and the evil spirits. Rather, all the positive things in the universe are shadows of Christ.

All the trees are shadows of Christ. In the Scriptures many trees are types of Christ, such as the tree of life (Gen. 2:9), the apple tree (S. S. 2:3), the cedar tree (5:15), and the fir tree (Hosea 14:8). The most significant tree is the vine tree mentioned in John 15. Christ is also the Root of David (Rev. 5:5) and the branch of Jesse (Isa. 11:1). A tree gives us fruit and shade. If we take the time to study how trees are used to illustrate Christ, we will see that Christ is everything. Many items of clothing also typify Christ. The garments of the high priest with their many details are a type of Christ. The many items of food also typify Christ. All the items on Solomon's feasting table and the items in his storage typify Christ (1 Kings 4:22-23). We should read the Scriptures in the way of seeing all the types and shadows of Christ.

Colossians shows us that God has made Christ to be everything. He is God Himself, and He is man. He is the Creator, and He is a creature. He accomplished redemption, and He is the Firstborn from the dead. He is the Head of the church, and He is even the Body. Christ is everything! In order to see this, we need Colossians. If we remove this book from the Bible, no one could understand Christ in such a profound way. If there were no Colossians, and I told you that Christ is everything, even the reality of the trees in the Bible, you may think I am foolish. If some would try to discover all the items mentioned in the Scriptures about Christ, they may not be able to finish the list in their lifetime. We praise the Lord that we have this book that shows us that Christ is everything.

CHRIST HAVING THE FIRST PLACE IN ALL THINGS

The fourth main point in Colossians is that Christ has the first place, the preeminence, in all things (1:18). That Christ would be the first in everything is according to God's plan.

CHRIST OUR PORTION

The fifth main point is that Christ is our portion. Colossians 1:12 says, "Giving thanks to the Father, who has qualified you for a share of the allotted portion of the saints in the light." Christ is the allotted portion given to us by God. Strictly speaking, God has given only Christ to us. All other things are simply shadows. No doubt God gives us food, sunshine, air, breath, and many good things, but all these things are merely shadows of Christ; the reality is Christ Himself. Christ is our portion.

In the entire universe what else is our portion? If we do not have Christ, we have nothing. Although we do have the shadows, they are vanity, because it is easy for shadows to depart. Even if we had a palace, in only one night it could burn up in a fire or be brought down by an earthquake. Everything soon fades away because it is all a shadow. Only Christ is the reality. Only He exists forever without change.

At the present time I am almost sixty years of age. I can say from my heart that I love nothing else. Only Him do I love. All night and all day I love Him. Nothing is so dear to me as He is. During the past half century from my teenage years to the present time, I have noticed all the changes in international and national affairs, in families, and in society. Everything is a shadow that passes away quickly. From this I have learned that nothing on earth is lovable or trustworthy. Only One is so dear to me, and He is so real to me. In nothing or no one else can I put my trust; I can trust only Him. He is the reality, and He is our portion.

If you do not have Christ, you are a person of vanity, but if you have Christ, you are a person of reality; you have Him, and He is everything. I hope that we all would learn to realize Him and love Him. Simply love Him, and do not seek anything else. Everything else is merely a shadow. Of course, while we are still on this earth, we need many things. However, we must use these things in the way of realizing Christ as our reality. The only portion which God gives to us is this wonderful Christ. We must learn to know Him, to live Him, to take Him, to experience Him, and to realize Him. He is not a religion, a doctrine, a set of teachings, or even Christianity, but an all-inclusive, real, and living Christ. It is worthwhile for us to have Him, and we can never regret having Him. Since my youth, for more than forty years, I have loved Him without any regret. He is the portion of the saints in the light.

CHRIST OUR LIFE

Sixth, this very Christ is life to us (3:4). He is very intimate, tender, subjective, and near. Nothing is as dear, precious, and available to us as our life, yet even our own life, the very life we received from our parents, is not the real life. It is only a shadow. Therefore, he who does not have Christ does not have the life (1 John 5:12). He is not only our portion for us to enjoy, but He is our life for us to live.

Even though I have been teaching and ministering for more than thirty years, I still do not have the adequate words to explain what it means that Christ is our life. This is something beyond human expression and human utterance. I can simply say that this wonderful Christ today is life to us. How precious and how wonderful this is! Christ is everything, He is our portion, and even more He is our life. In all the sixty-six books of the Bible, Colossians 3:4 is the clearest word about Christ being our life.

CHRIST AS OUR EVERYTHING

The last main point concerns Christ being everything to us. Christ is not only everything, but everything to us. We must learn how to experience Christ as everything to us. Christ to us is our food and drink, and He is also our patience. Many times we are short of patience. When we are short of patience, we should realize that we are actually short of Christ. Christ is our patience. Do we desire humility? Christ Himself is our humility. Do we want to honor our father and our mother? The honor that we render to our father and mother must be Christ. Christ is even the way for us to honor our parents. There is no need for teaching concerning the way. If we love Christ and fellowship with Him, we will have Christ as the living way. We will know how to honor our parents, and Christ will become the strength for us to honor our parents. Christ is everything to us.

I believe that in these last days the Lord will recover His people to know Him not merely in doctrine but in a very experiential way. When we write a letter to a friend, our letter must be Christ. We must learn to experience Christ in such a way. Before we write the letter, we should fellowship with the Lord and be one with Him. We must tell Him, "Lord, You Yourself must be my words. I will not write anything besides Yourself to my friend. What I am going to write must be You." We must try to experience the Lord in this way, applying Him as everything in our daily life. He must be everything to us. When we minister the word, that word must be Christ. Our message and ministry must be Christ, and the way to minister and our strength to minister must be Christ. The book of Colossians was written because many of those believers did not know how to experience Christ in such a way. They were distracted from Christ to pay attention to other things. Colossians was written to tell them that they must realize Christ as their everything. We also must learn to experience Christ in such a real and living way. Even from our youth, we should begin to experience Christ. I thank the Lord that I was saved as a young man. However, I did not receive the proper help. I received great help in studying the Bible according to the letter, but I was not helped to know the Lord in a living way, to experience Him as my life and everything. After about seven or eight years passed, I began to receive help in knowing Christ in a living way. Praise the Lord that many of you who are still in your teenage years can receive this help now! You should not take this in a light way. You should appreciate that you are being shown the way to take Christ, experience Him, and apply Him as everything. I hope that the younger generation will pay their full attention to this matter. Then they will be the living witnesses, the living testimonies, of how dear, how real, how precious, how rich, and how living Christ is. Let us learn to experience Him in this way.

CHAPTER TWENTY

CHRIST AS EVERYTHING IN COLOSSIANS

(2)

Scripture Reading: Col. 2:6-8; 1:9-11; 2:11-12; 3:1, 3, 9-11;
1:27; 2:16-17, 19

RECEIVING CHRIST

In the previous chapter we saw seven main points in
Colossians. The next main point is that we receive Christ.
Colossians 2:6 begins, "As therefore you have received the
Christ, Jesus the Lord." *Received* is a very meaningful and
important word. Only two books, the Gospel of John and
Colossians, speak of receiving Christ in this way. John 1:12
says, "But as many as received Him." When I was young I did
not properly understand the meaning of believing in the Lord
Jesus. However, after many years I realized that to believe in
the Lord Jesus simply means to receive the Lord Jesus, like a
radio receives the radio waves in the air and people receive
breath into their bodies. Colossians stresses that we have
received Christ.

WALKING IN CHRIST

The ninth main point in Colossians is that we walk in
Christ. Colossians 2:6 concludes by saying, "Walk in Him."
This verse tells us to walk not according to Him but in Him.
In Him means that Christ is a sphere, a realm in which we
walk, signified by the good land of Canaan. *In Him* also
includes the meaning of walking by Him, just as travelling in
a car means that we travel by the car.

Rejecting Human Philosophies
and Distracting Teachings

In the early days of the church, the Colossian believers were confused and carried away from the knowledge of Christ. According to church history, they were distracted by Gnosticism, a philosophy composed of Jewish, Egyptian, Persian, and Greek teachings. Those teachings appeared to be good, in the same way the teachings of Confucius appear to be good. The word *Gnosticism* itself indicates the word of knowledge and wisdom. Verse 8 speaks of philosophy; in writing this, Paul had in mind Gnosticism, the teaching and thoughts of human wisdom. He also speaks of the elements of the world, the rudimentary teachings of the world. This also is related to the teaching of the Gnostics. This Gnostic philosophy was brought into the church and caused confusion regarding the proper knowledge of Christ. Hence, many believers were distracted from experiencing Christ. This was the reason that Paul wrote Colossians.

The principle of this portion of the Word is that throughout all the centuries there have always been good teachings invented and taught by man that distract Christians from the real knowledge and experience of Christ. In China, for example, many Christians were distracted by the ethical teachings of Confucius from the real and living experience of Christ. We must realize that when we were regenerated, we received Christ as our life and our everything, so Christ has become the sphere, the realm, and the means for us to live on the earth and walk in the presence of God. Therefore, we must reject and abandon not only the bad things but even the good things, the best teachings invented by man.

The best thing invented by man in human culture and civilization is not science. Many times science has produced awful things, such as machines to kill many people. The best human invention is philosophy. However, we must never be distracted by human philosophy; it is a subtle substitute for Christ. Satan uses philosophy in a subtle way to distract people from the real experience of Christ, but many times we do not realize that we have been distracted. We may consider that philosophy is good because it helps us to be better persons, to have a better living, which is a glory to God. This is wrong. We Christians have received Christ as our life and as our everything, and now we must learn not to know any good thing other than Christ. We should abandon all the other good things and learn to live and walk in Christ. I would caution the young brothers and sisters about studying books of philosophy. I do not like to see that a young person would major in philosophy at a university. To do this is to put yourself into the mouth of a tiger; at any time the enemy, Satan, can swallow you. Human philosophy is very deceiving for Christians.

Our Need for a Detailed Experience of Christ in Our Daily Life

The basic principle in Colossians is that God has given Christ to us. According to Colossians, the will of God is to make Christ everything to us, to give us Christ as our portion, our life, and our everything. By the mercy and grace of God we have received Christ as the all-inclusive One. Therefore, after we receive Him, we must walk in Him as our sphere and by Him as our means. We must learn to know Christ in this way.

We should not think that since we have heard this word and read Colossians, that we know everything. What we are speaking here may be considered as instructions telling us that we need to know Christ and walk in Him. Now we must learn these things through our daily experience. I am saddened by the fact that not many Christians have learned how to experience Christ in a detailed way in their daily life. I have heard certain teachings about this, but I have not met many Christians who practice the real experience of Christ in their daily life. Today what we need is not more good teachings but to learn to live by Him in a practical way. All the good teachings other than Christ should be put aside. We must spend more time to know Christ, not merely by our understanding but by the wisdom in our spirit.

Knowing Christ in All Spiritual Wisdom and Understanding

The apostle Paul gives us the secret and the way to walk in

Christ in 1:9-11. Verse 9 says, "Therefore we also, since the day we heard of it, do not cease praying and asking on your behalf that you may be filled with the full knowledge of His will in all spiritual wisdom and understanding." In order to experience Christ and walk in Christ, we must have all spiritual wisdom and understanding. We need the wisdom in our spirit to realize Christ. First of all, we must realize that in God's purpose, His will is to make Christ everything to us. We must have a clear understanding of this. To be sure, in order to experience Christ, we have to know Him. The more we know and realize Him, the more we sense that we need Him, and the more we are willing to experience Him. Therefore, we need spiritual wisdom and understanding, that is, the revelation and vision concerning Christ. Hence, we need to read the Scriptures to gain the knowledge of Christ. However, we should not read merely in the way of mental understanding in letter. Rather, whenever we read the things concerning Christ in the record of the Scriptures, we must pray much.

Knowing Christ by Exercising Our Spirit in the Word

We should not merely exercise our mentality to understand the Bible in its black and white letters. Of course, we need understanding. If we do not understand English, for example, we can never understand an English version of the Bible. We must know the words and understand them with our mind. However, this is not all. After we understand the words, we must immediately exercise our spirit. This requires much prayer. We may illustrate this by eating. When we eat, it is important to thoroughly chew our food. The more time we spend to chew the food, the more we get the nourishment and the easier it is to digest it. Chewing food illustrates the way to read the Word with the exercise of the spirit. After we see the words, read the words, and understand them, we need to "chew" them. This is done not by our understanding but by our prayer.

For this reason we need to exercise our spirit. When we read, we need to exercise our mind to understand the words, and we may even need to go to a dictionary. However, after we understand the words, we need to exercise our spirit and pray from the spirit: "Lord, I open my mouth. I wish to sense Your word from the depths of my spirit." In this way the secrets of the Word will be opened to us. We will pass through the surface of the black and white letters and find the depths. Then we will see something different and living. At this time we will know Christ not merely according to the letter but according to spiritual understanding and realization. We will receive the vision and revelation of Christ from the Word. We all need to read the Word in this way.

We may illustrate the way to eat the Word with Colossians 2:16-17. In the previous chapter we saw that eating, drinking, the feasts, and the Sabbath are a shadow of the things to come, but the body is of Christ. In reading these verses, we must first know the meaning of the words in black and white. Following this, we need to pray in order to exercise our spirit to realize the spiritual matters, the spiritual content in this word. Then something will be opened to us, not only something of the Word but something of Christ Himself. We will realize that what we need is Christ as the reality. We all need to have the spiritual wisdom and understanding so that we may realize Christ. Then we will be able to experience Him.

Walking according to the Revelation of Christ

Colossians 1:10 says, "To walk worthily of the Lord to please Him in all things, bearing fruit in every good work and growing by the full knowledge of God." To walk worthily of the Lord and grow by the full knowledge of God is to live and walk according to spiritual wisdom and understanding. After we receive the revelation and vision concerning Christ, we have to walk according to it. Then we will walk worthily of the Lord and partake of the Lord more and more. In this way we grow by Christ being increased in us. The way for Christ to increase in us is by our receiving spiritual wisdom, understanding, and revelation concerning Christ and by walking according to the spiritual revelation of Christ that we have received. This is to gain the real, subjective, and experiential knowledge of God, by which we grow with the increase of Christ.

Being Empowered with All Power

Verse 11 says, "Being empowered with all power, according to the might of His glory, unto all endurance and long-suffering with joy." We need the inner empowering according to the might of His glory. This is not only to have revelation in our understanding; it is something more. It is that the Holy Spirit within us strengthens us, energizes us, and imparts the might of God's glory into us.

First we have revelation and vision in our spiritual understanding. Then, we make the decision to walk according to that vision. Third, we look to the Lord that He may strengthen us with His power. This is the proper way to walk in Christ.

ROOTED AND BUILT UP IN CHRIST

The tenth main point in Colossians is found in 2:7, which says, "Having been rooted and being built up in Him." *Having been rooted* and *being built up* are different verb tenses. Our being rooted is already accomplished, but our being built up is a process. We have been rooted in Christ. There is no need for us to be rooted again because this has already been accomplished. What we need now is to be built up.

To be built up has two meanings. On the one hand, we ourselves need to be built up with Christ just as a little child needs to be built up into an adult. Although we have been rooted in Christ, the measure of Christ within us may be small; we may not have an adequate measure of Christ. If we are built up with Christ, we will have a proper measure of Christ within us. On the other hand, we need to be built up with others. Colossians emphasizes Christ as the Head of the Body. All the members themselves must be built up, and they must also be built together as the Body.

The second aspect of building depends on the first. If we ourselves have not been built up, how can we be built together with others? To be built together with others depends on our being built up. Our growing in Christ is a matter not only of receiving Christ and walking in Him but of being built up ourselves and being built up with others. These are very important matters with many details.

To be rooted in Christ means that we are plants who have been put in Christ as our soil. Therefore, we must enjoy Christ, experience Him, and be built up in Him. In order to build, we need materials. As we are plants, Christ is the soil to us, and as we are the building, He is the very material with which we are built. An American child is built up by eating the produce of America, such as beef, chicken, fish, and fruit. In the same way, our spiritual measure is built up by feeding on Christ. At present we may have a small spiritual measure. We need to grow to a greater measure of Christ, and the way to grow in measure is by feeding on Christ, taking Him in, and digesting Him. Then He will be added to us more and more. We will have Christ increased within us, and our measure will grow. Christ is the material for the building up of our spiritual measure. For us to be rooted, Christ is the soil, and for us to be built up, Christ is the material. Christ is the very substance, element, and material for us to grow and be built up.

We have received Christ. Now we need to walk in Him and by Him. In order to walk in Him, we need to know Him in revelation and vision, and after we receive the revelation, we have to walk according to what we see. Then we open to Him and allow the Holy Spirit to strengthen us into our spirit, imparting the might of His glory into us that we might be empowered to walk in Christ. Then we must realize that we have been rooted in Christ. Christ is the very source of our supply, and as the soil He is our entire supply. From Christ as the soil we absorb all the supply we need to grow. He is the very material, substance, and element with which we can have a greater measure in spirit. All this in total is the growth of Christ. I hope that you will spend time to bring these matters to the Lord, to pray about them, and to learn to practice them. We must realize all these matters and put them into practice. Then we will have the real experience of Christ. We will then be able to help others, not merely to teach them about Christ but to minister to them the living knowledge and experience of Christ.

IDENTIFIED WITH CHRIST TO BE THE NEW MAN

The next main point in Colossians is our identification with Christ. We are identified with Christ in four things—in His death, in His burial, in His resurrection, and in His ascension (2:11-12; 3:1, 3). We died with Christ, we were buried with Him, we were raised with Him, and we ascended with Him. Therefore, we are no longer the old man but the new man (vv. 9-10). In our daily walk we must always reject the old man and everything of the old man as that which is dead and buried and has nothing to do with us any more. We are now resurrected and ascended with Christ in the heavens, and we are the members of the new man. Within this new man there is nothing old. There cannot be Greek and Jew, circumcision and uncircumcision, barbarian, Scythian, slave, or free man (v. 11). All these are the old things. In the new man everything is Christ. Christ is all and in all.

We are now in the new man, so we must put on the new man in our experience. We realize that we have been united and identified with Christ; we are dead, buried, resurrected, and ascended in Him and with Him. Therefore, all the things of the old man have nothing to do with us; we put them off and reckon them as buried. Then we live in the new man and walk as the new man. In this way we enjoy Christ not only by ourselves but by and in the corporate Body, which is the church, the new man.

CHRIST IN US, THE HOPE OF GLORY

The twelfth main point in Colossians is found in 1:27. Christ in us is the hope of glory. He is not only our life but also our hope, which is the hope of glory. *Hope of glory* indicates that when Christ comes, He will bring us into glory, that is, He will glorify us. Today this glory is concealed by our physical body, but one day when He comes, our physical body will be changed in nature by being transfigured. The glory which is Christ Himself as life will shine out through our body to bring our entire body and our entire person into glory. We should not think that glory is something objective that will come upon us some day. Rather, this glory is subjectively within us today, and one day it will spread out through our body. The divine life will swallow up the death within us, and we will be in glory.

Through transfiguration our body will become transparent, like the shade of an electric lamp. One day the Lord will come to transfigure the "lampshade" and make it transparent. Then the glory within will shine out, and the "lampshade" will be in glory. This will transpire on the day of our glorification, but today the glory is already within us. Christ in us is the hope of glory.

THE WAY TO APPLY CHRIST

Another main point in Colossians is the way to apply Christ. The main goal of this book is to tell us how to apply Christ and appropriate Him. This entire book is a book of application, telling us how to appropriate Christ in our daily life in order to meet our every need. Colossians 1:12 tells us that Christ is the portion of the saints, but we must know how to enjoy and apply Him. In the early days of the church some of the Christians in Colossae had a Jewish background. They regarded special foods and drinks and observed the Old Testament feasts, the new moons, and the Sabbath. The apostle Paul told them that these items were only a shadow and that they must give them up. Christ is the very body of the shadow (2:16-17). They needed to apply Christ as the real food, drink, days of feast, new moons, and Sabbath. By this passage alone we can realize that the intention of this book is to show us our need to appropriate Christ in a practical way, even in our eating and drinking.

THE INCREASE OF GOD FOR THE GROWTH AND BUILDING UP OF THE BODY

The last main point is found in 2:19, which is an important verse. This verse says, "Holding the Head, out from whom all the Body, being richly supplied and knit together by means of the joints and sinews, grows with the growth of God." Joints are for supplying the nourishment needed by the Body, and sinews are for knitting the members of the Body together. Among the believers, some are joints that nourish and supply, while others are sinews that join, unite, and knit the members together. By this nourishment and knitting the Body receives the supply from the Head, and it grows with the growth of God. This means that God increases within us, because what we receive from Christ the Head is something of God, even the fullness of the Godhead. On the one hand, the growth of the Body is the increase of the element of Christ within us, while on the other hand, it is the increase of God Himself. In this way the Body grows.

We may compare this to the growth of a tree. A tree grows by the fertilizer. As we put fertilizer into the soil, the tree absorbs more riches from the soil. Because the tree has more elements and more nourishment, it grows by this element and nourishment. As members of the Body, what we receive from Christ the Head is the very fullness and essence of God. The more we receive Christ, the more we have the increase of God, and it is by this increase that the Body grows and is built up.

These fourteen main points cover the entire book of Colossians. By such a book we can know Christ in a full way, and we can know who Christ is. We can know the Head of the universal man, and we can know how to appropriate Him in our daily lives. We can know how to receive, enjoy, and experience Christ so that the essence of God will constantly increase and we will have more and more of God. In this way the Body will grow and be built up. We need to "chew" and digest all the important points of this book. Then they will become our experience.

CHAPTER TWENTY-ONE

FAITH, LOVE, AND HOPE
IN 1 AND 2 THESSALONIANS

Scripture Reading: 1 Thes. 1:10; 2:19-20; 3:13; 4:17-18; 5:23; 2 Thes. 2:1-8; 1 Thes. 1:3; 2 Thes. 1:3; 1 Tim. 1:5; 2 Pet. 1:1, 3-7

Among all the Epistles written by the apostle Paul, the two to the Thessalonians are the simplest, and they are among the earliest. Why then are these two Epistles placed toward the end of his fourteen Epistles in the arrangement of the New Testament? I believe that the sovereignty of God is in this arrangement.

In the previous messages of this series we have seen a full definition of the universal man. We have clearly and thoroughly seen Christ as the Head, the church as the Body, and the way that the members of this Body should walk and live. Now after the definition of the universal man in the foregoing books of the New Testament, 1 and 2 Thessalonians show us an additional matter, the coming of the Lord. These two books are found at this juncture because the second coming of Christ is the consummation of the life of the universal man. Christ's coming is the consummation of the Christian life, the Christian walk, and the church life.

A BALANCED VIEW OF THE LORD'S SECOND COMING

These two books are arranged in a very meaningful order. Since both speak about the coming of the Lord, why is there the need of two books to relate this matter? Why is one epistle not adequate? One of the best ways to study the Word is to compare two books, two chapters, two passages, two verses, or even two words. With all the matters revealed in the

Scripture, there are always two aspects, two sides. It is a principle that for anything in the universe to exist, it must have two sides. Nothing can exist with only one side. Even a thin piece of paper has two sides. For example, there are the heavens and the earth, God and man, man and woman, inside and outside, and top and bottom. In our own physical body, most of its members are in pairs. We have two ears, two eyes, two arms, two hands, two legs, and so forth. This provides balance. If we had only one leg, we could not stand for long because we would lack balance. Medical doctors tell us that our two ears are also for balance.

The two books to the Thessalonians show us the coming of the Lord in a balanced way. The first book encourages the saints by the coming of the Lord. The coming of the Lord means very much to us. It is our hope, our encouragement, our comfort, and our strength. To those early Christians also, the Lord's second coming meant very much. However, whenever we are encouraged by a hope, it is easy to go too far. We may say that since the Lord will come tomorrow, we can forget about everything else. This is wrong, unbalanced, and to an extreme. Therefore, we need the second epistle to tell us the other side. Hence, the second epistle is a balance to the first one. This is the main reason that there are two epistles concerning the Lord's coming. If we read them carefully, we will see the balance.

The Encouragement in the First Epistle

No other book of the sixty-six books of the Bible is composed in the way that 1 Thessalonians is. Every chapter of this epistle ends with the coming of the Lord. The last verse of chapter one says, "Await His Son from the heavens" (v. 10). This is the coming of the Lord. At the end of chapter two, verses 19-20 say, "For what is our hope or joy or crown of boasting before our Lord Jesus at His coming? Are not even you? For you are our glory and joy." The last verse in chapter three says, "So that He may establish your hearts blameless in holiness before our God and Father at the coming of our Lord Jesus with all His saints" (v. 13). Chapter four ends clearly with the subject of the Lord's coming: "Then we who are living, who are left remaining, will be caught up together with them in the clouds to meet the Lord in the air; and thus we will be always with the Lord. Therefore comfort one another with these words" (vv. 17-18). Finally, 5:23 says, "And the God of peace Himself sanctify you wholly, and may your spirit and soul and body be preserved complete, without blame, at the coming of our Lord Jesus Christ."

Every chapter ends with the coming of the Lord because this is a crucial matter in this book. In chapter one the writer talks about the Christian walk; then he encourages the believers with the coming of the Lord. Then, in chapter two Paul teaches us about the fostering of the believers, and he ends this section with the coming of the Lord as an encouragement. Chapter three is the same in principle, and in chapter four Paul gives comfort by speaking about the coming of the Lord Jesus to the saints who had lost some of their hope. Again in chapter five Paul encourages the saints by the coming of the Lord Jesus. First Thessalonians is a book of encouragement by the coming of the Lord. In his earliest epistle Paul uses the coming of the Lord to encourage the believers to go on.

No doubt all those Christians were encouraged by Paul's word. They may have exclaimed, "This is glorious! The Lord is coming. Everything is for this, so let us forget about everything else." Bible teachers agree that after Paul's first epistle, certain others took advantage of this opportunity to say that the Lord Jesus would come back very soon, even after only a few days. It seems that such ones spoke the same thing as the apostle Paul, but in actuality they did not. Although the apostle used the Lord's second coming as an encouragement in his first epistle, some people misused it. Therefore, the second epistle was written to balance them.

The Balance in the Second Epistle

Second Thessalonians 2:1-2 says, "Now we ask you, brothers, with regard to the coming of our Lord Jesus Christ and our gathering together to Him, that you be not quickly shaken in mind nor alarmed, neither by a spirit nor by word nor by a letter as if by us, to the effect that the day of the Lord has come." This suggests that after Paul's first letter, others who seemed to agree with the apostle wrote to say something extreme about the Lord's second coming. The news concerning this must have come to the apostle, who then wrote the second epistle to adjust, correct, and balance the believers.

Verses 3-8 continue, "Let no one deceive you in any way, because it will not come unless the apostasy comes first and the man of lawlessness is revealed, the son of perdition, who opposes and exalts himself above all that is called God or an object of worship, so that he sits in the temple of God, setting himself forth, saying that he is God. Do you not remember that while I was still with you, I said these things to you? And now you know that which restrains, so that he might be revealed in his own time. For it is the mystery of lawlessness that is now operating, but only until the one now restraining goes out of the way. And then the lawless one will be revealed (whom the Lord Jesus will slay by the breath of His mouth and bring to nothing by the manifestation of His coming)."

If we read this word carefully, we can realize that it is a correction, a judgment, and a balance for the extreme teaching. The believers had been encouraged by Paul's word concerning the coming of the Lord, but they were pushed too far. No doubt, the Lord Jesus will come back, but there is still the need to be balanced. Throughout the centuries Christians have made many mistakes concerning the Lord's coming simply because they neglected to be balanced. On the one hand, we must believe and admit that the Lord Jesus is coming quickly, but on the other hand, we need to realize that prior to the Lord's coming a number of events must happen. Unless these things transpire first, it is impossible for the Lord to come back. This is the balance.

Our hope as Christians is the second coming of the Lord Jesus, but some people believe in the Lord's coming in an unbalanced way. According to the history of the church, people have said many foolish things concerning the Lord's second coming because they neglected the second aspect, the aspect that certain things must first be fulfilled. However, there are also many believers who overstress the second aspect when they study the different signs related to the end times. The second coming of Christ is a big subject and to study it requires much time. I studied the different schools concerning the second coming and the rapture. I studied the Brethren teachings and those of G. H. Pember and D. M. Panton. The Brethren especially spent a great amount of time studying the signs. I was with the Brethren for seven years and studied the signs with them. I heard more than one hundred messages concerning the seventy weeks in Daniel 9. They always spoke of the seven weeks, the sixty-two weeks, and the last week divided into two halves of three and a half years, or forty-two months, or one thousand two hundred sixty days. Even until today I can remember all those details. Because of these teachings, however, many have become lazy. They can sleep well and rise late, being sure that the Lord Jesus cannot come back yet because all the signs have not been fulfilled.

THE WORK OF FAITH, LABOR OF LOVE, AND ENDURANCE OF HOPE

In the first Epistle to the Thessalonians there are three words which are very important—faith, love, and hope. Verse 3 of chapter one says, "Remembering unceasingly your work of faith and labor of love and endurance of hope in our Lord Jesus Christ, before our God and Father." Faith relates mainly to the past, although we still need faith at the present time. The Christian life is initiated by faith; faith is the starting point of the Christian life. Following this, love is the present process of the Christian life, and hope is for the future. A proper Christian life is a life of faith as the start, love in the process, and hope for the future. These three are all related. If we are short of any one of these three, our Christian life has a problem.

Anything solid must have three dimensions. If something has three dimensions, it is established, solid, and stable. When the ancient Jews constructed a building, for example, they laid the foundation stone, built the structure upon it, and placed a topstone, a crowning stone, to complete and cover it. Faith, love, and hope are the three dimensions of the Christian walk. Faith is the foundation, love is the structure, and hope is the topstone. A solid Christian life must be a life of love, but love is founded on faith and has hope as its covering.

In all our work and living we must have love, which issues out
of and is produced by faith (1 Tim. 1:5, 14; 2:15; 2 Tim. 1:13;
Gal. 5:6).

We must keep these three items in mind—faith, love, and
hope—when we read 1 and 2 Thessalonians. These eight
chapters are a development of the three dimensions of the
Christian walk. It is not necessary to expound every verse in
these books; if we remember that these two books deal with
these three dimensions, we will understand all eight chapters.

We pursue the Lord day by day because He has given us
faith. However, this faith causes us trouble. If the Lord had
not given us faith, we could go along in a fallen way and still
be at peace, but since the day we received faith, we have been
troubled by it. It is this living faith, this saving faith, that not
only turns us back to the Lord but also encourages us to go on.
There is something within us that always stirs us up and
encourages us to be active. We may say that this is the Lord
Jesus, but we should also say that it is this wonderful faith
within us.

Second Peter 1:1 says, "Simon Peter, a slave and apostle of
Jesus Christ, to those who have been allotted faith equally
precious as ours in the righteousness of our God and Savior,
Jesus Christ." This verse says that we obtain faith in the righteousness of God, but Romans and Galatians tell us that we
obtain righteousness through faith (Rom. 4:5, 13; 9:30; 10:6;
Gal. 3:5-6). Does faith come first or righteousness? The
answer is that faith is a seed sown into us that grows. Second
Peter 1:3-7 continues, "Seeing that His divine power has
granted to us all things which relate to life and godliness...through which He has granted to us precious and
exceedingly great promises that through these you might
become partakers of the divine nature....And for this very
reason also, adding all diligence, supply bountifully in your
faith virtue; and in virtue, knowledge; and in knowledge,
self-control; and in self-control, endurance; and in endurance,
godliness; and in godliness, brotherly love; and in brotherly
love, love." To faith are added more and more virtues until
eventually love is added in two aspects—love for the brothers

and love for all people. This sequence begins with faith and ends with love. This is the proper growth in the Christian life.

Faith as the foundation within us causes us to live a certain kind of life. On the one hand, faith as a seed sown into us is a foundation to strengthen us, while on the other hand, this living and dynamic faith constantly troubles us. If there were no faith within us, not one of us would remain in the church life. We would run to the beach, to the movies, or go dancing. However, if we go to the beach or to the movies, we do not have the peace within. Something within rises up to ask, "Is this eternal? Is this divine?" We may want to find a better job, but the faith within us may not agree. If we pursue a Ph.D. or seek to be a bank manager, something within may ask, "Is this for the Lord Jesus? Is this eternal and divine? Is this precious in the eyes of God?" This troubling element is the faith within us. Faith within us always troubles us and keeps us from the worldly things.

As a result, love follows this living faith. We may tell the Lord with tears, "Lord, I love You. I forsake myself. I give up all the glory of this age. For Your sake I would stop seeking the worldly things. I just love You. I want to spend my time and energy and be spent to gain souls for You. I desire to serve You, to work for You, and to live for You because I love You." This is the labor of love. What bubbles up, rises up, and is produced by living faith is a sweet love. Although many times we are suffering or persecuted and have many problems, we sense a sweetness toward the Lord. Sometimes with tears we may say, "Lord, I praise You, and I really love You," and the more we tell the Lord that we love Him, the more our tears come. This is love as a product of faith. Love carries us on to work for the Lord, to live for the Lord, to go along with the Lord, and even to sacrifice our life as martyrs for the Lord. This love comes from faith.

Moreover, this love has a crown, a topstone, which is hope. Whenever we say that we love the Lord, spontaneously and unconsciously within us there is a hope to see Him. Whenever we say, "Lord, I am living for You because I love You," spontaneously hope rises up within us. We have the hope of seeing Him and meeting Him. Very often we cannot and would not do certain things, and we determine to not be defeated, simply because we realize that we will see the Lord. We must stand and fight the battle to the end because one day, perhaps tomorrow, we will meet Him. This is our hope.

The entire Christian life and walk is built with these three dimensions—faith as the foundation, love as the structure, and hope as the topstone. The two epistles to the Thessalonians are a development, definition, and explanation of the work of faith, the labor of love, and the endurance of hope, and we can understand all eight chapters in this light.

ENCOURAGED BY THE COMING OF CHRIST WHILE WORKING IN A FAITHFUL WAY

First and 2 Thessalonians particularly stress the last dimension—hope—more than the other two. Whatever we are and whatever we do must be in the light of the coming of the Lord. As the members of the Body, the church, we must live in the light of the Lord's coming. As the church, the corporate Body, we must exist in the light of the Lord's coming. If one is an apostle, he must be an apostle in the light of the Lord's coming. If one is a minister of the word, he must minister in the light of the Lord's coming. This is the third dimension of the Christian walk. This is the reason that the second coming of the Lord is mentioned at the end of every chapter of 1 Thessalonians. The apostle Paul composed all the matters of the Christian life in the light of the Lord's coming.

However, we should not be an unturned cake, burned on one side but raw on the other (Hosea 7:8). We need to be balanced. To be sure, the coming of the Lord is an encouragement to us, but we should not take this encouragement improperly, believing that since the Lord is coming soon we can do things irresponsibly. This is wrong. We must still do things in a proper way. On the one hand, we realize that the Lord is coming, and we are encouraged by this. On the other hand, we must realize that the Lord may not come right away. He may delay His coming, so there is still time left for us to do His work faithfully and properly. We should be faithful, honest, and diligent to do our duty, being encouraged by His coming.

At all times we must be encouraged by the Lord's coming. We need to be reminded that one day we will see Him. Regardless of how much we suffer for Him and lose for Him, His coming is a comfort to us. However, we must not receive this comfort in the way of neglecting our duty, our ministry. We must not think that since the Lord is coming for us, we can waste our days in a loose and light way. We are encouraged by the Lord's coming, but we realize that the Lord still gives us the time to do things in a proper way. We must be balanced in these two aspects of the Lord's coming.

THE PAROUSIA OF CHRIST

Second Thessalonians 2:1 says, "Now we ask you, brothers, with regard to the coming of our Lord Jesus Christ and our gathering together to Him." *Coming* is a key word. This is not the ordinary word for *coming* in Greek. It is the Greek word *parousia,* meaning "presence." From Matthew through Revelation, this word is often used in the passages that relate to the Lord's coming. If we do not know the proper meaning and usage of this word, we can never understand the Lord's coming in an accurate way. All the verses in the Bible relating to the Lord's second coming are like pieces of a jigsaw puzzle, and without this key word we would not know how to put the pieces together.

When we speak of the Lord's coming, our human thought is that He will come back suddenly at a definite hour. However, the Lord's parousia, His presence, is not something that comes all of a sudden. By the study of the entire New Testament, we know that the Lord's parousia will last for a certain period of time. It will not be only a day or a month; it will probably last for a period of a few years. Certain passages of the Scriptures indicate that His parousia will be before the great tribulation, others indicate that it will be during the tribulation, while other verses show us that it will be at the end of the tribulation. If we put all these puzzle pieces together, we can see the full picture. The parousia of the Lord will not come suddenly and then vanish. It will last for a certain period of time.

In Matthew 24:36 the Lord says clearly that no one knows the time of His parousia except the Father. According to this word, the day of the Lord's parousia is a secret that no one knows, a secret kept in the mind of God the Father until a certain time that we do not know. Second Thessalonians 2:3-4, however, tells us that the day of the Lord comes after the man of lawlessness, Antichrist, is revealed and does certain things. According to this word, the day of the Lord's coming can be determined. On the one hand, the Scriptures indicate that we can determine the time of the day of the Lord, while on the other hand, the Lord Himself tells us that no one knows the day. Seemingly this is a contradiction, but in actuality it is not. Whereas no one can know the time of the beginning of the Lord's parousia, the end of His parousia can be determined by signs. No one knows when the Lord's parousia will begin, but by signs in the future, the signs to come, we can calculate when the Lord's parousia will end.

This should cause us to be watchful. We should not say that since we have not yet seen the signs, the Lord's coming will not be soon. This is only one aspect. We must take care of the other aspect. The Lord's parousia can begin at any time without signs; therefore, we must be watchful. His parousia will be like a thief in the night who comes without giving notice. When a thief comes, he does not make a telephone call to say when he will come. A thief comes mainly when people are not ready. No one can determine when the Lord's parousia will begin. Therefore, we must be warned to be watchful. We cannot be sloppy or loose. We have to be watchful because at any time the Lord's parousia may begin.

WALKING, WORKING, AND LIVING
IN THE LIGHT OF THE LORD'S COMING

The main emphasis of the two books to the Thessalonians is that the Christian walk and living is one of three dimensions—faith, love, and hope. Faith is the beginning as the foundation, the source; love is the process as the structure, the main part; and hope is the end, the consummation. We must always begin by faith. Then, we must walk, live, work, and do things for the Lord in love with the hope that one day we will meet Him. We will see Him, and He will see us. What a wonderful and glorious day that will be! Yet we have to be warned. What will happen if we are not faithful to Him? This is a warning to us.

There is no need to explain and define all eight chapters of these two books. If we keep all the above main points in mind when we read them, we will receive the proper light. We will be warned and reminded, and we will learn to be watchful, to go on with the Lord based upon faith, in the process of love, and with the hope of His coming. We should not care how much we suffer or lose for Him, because we know that we will see Him. Every kind of trouble, persecution, and suffering will become a glory in His presence.

The purpose of these two books is to show us that we need to walk, work, and live in the light of the Lord's coming. His coming must always be before us. We dare not be defeated or love the world, the fleshy things, and the things of this age, because one day we have to meet Him. We also do not care about our suffering or loss because one day He will reward us in His presence. We must be the faithful ministers, faithful servants, faithful believers, and faithful members of His Body because one day we will stand before Him in His glory. This is the proper interpretation of these two books.

We should not use these two books to argue with people about doctrine. Rather, may the Lord be merciful that we would have the work of faith, the labor of love, and the endurance of hope. Endurance is a real strength to us. If we have endurance, we can do everything. Endurance comes from the hope of glory. We have the hope that we will see Him, that one day He will come, and that one day He and we will be in glory. By this we have endurance. This endurance is the power and strength for us to suffer, labor, press on, live for Him, and sacrifice everything for Him. Strength is in endurance, and endurance is in hope.

CHAPTER TWENTY-TWO

THE PRACTICE OF THE CHURCH LIFE
IN 1 AND 2 TIMOTHY

Scripture Reading: 1 Tim. 3:15-16; 4:7-8; 2 Tim. 2:2; 1 Tim.
1:5, 19; 4:2; 1:12; 6:12; 2 Tim. 4:1, 18, 7-8; 1 Tim. 1:14; 2 Tim.
4:22

The arrangement of the order of the Epistles of the New
Testament reveals the sovereignty of the Lord. By studying
these particular books carefully, we can realize that the Epistles, from Romans to Jude, are divided into two main groups.
The thirteen books from Romans to Philemon are the first
group, and the eight books from Hebrews to Jude are the
second group. The first group of Epistles gives a complete
structure of the definition of the Body of Christ, whereas the
second group serves as supplementary books. With good writings there is often the need of a supplement. The important
matters that are hard to position in the main line are placed
at the end in a supplement. The supplement is important and
necessary, but it is not in the main line that runs through the
writing.

ROMANS TO 2 THESSALONIANS BEING MAINLY ON LIFE

The first main group of Epistles, which speaks of the definition of the Body of Christ, is further divided into two
sections. The first section contains nine books, from Romans
to 2 Thessalonians. Then from 1 Timothy to Philemon there
are another four books forming a second section. The church
as the Body of Christ needs two things, life and practice. Even
our own physical body needs both life and exercise. For our
body to do anything, it first needs life. If the body does not
have life, it can do nothing. However, even if it has life, it still

needs proper exercise. In order to drive a car, for example, we need the human life. A dog or a cat with its own respective life can never drive a car. Only the higher life is adequate to drive a car. However, this does not mean that as long as we have the human life, we can drive a car. There is still the need of practice and exercise.

The first nine books in the first section, Romans to 2 Thessalonians, deal mostly with the life side. They tell us what the nature, life, function, responsibility, and consummation of the Body of Christ are. These five matters characterize the different aspects of the life side. These books tell us how we receive life, how life grows and works within us, and how this life with its nature enables us to function in the Body and bear responsibility. Lastly, the consummation of this life is the second coming of the Lord Jesus. This is all on the side of life.

FIRST TIMOTHY THROUGH PHILEMON BEING MAINLY ON PRACTICE

Following the life side, there is the side of practice and exercise. With life we need exercise, practice, and learning. After being taught and becoming experienced in practice, we must take the responsibility to teach others, because with life there must be practice, and practice includes teaching and learning. The four books from 1 Timothy through Philemon present practice with teaching and learning.

The Epistles from Romans to 2 Thessalonians seem to cover everything and be complete. They tell us how we were sinners condemned before God, how we were justified and saved, how originally we were dead but were regenerated and made alive, how we received Christ into us as our life, and how this life has a consummation. It seems that everything has been covered, and they are short of nothing. However, without 1 and 2 Timothy, Titus, and Philemon, we would have the life of the church, but we would not know how to practice the church life. We would not know, for example, how to have elders and deacons. To remove these four books from the Bible would be a great loss.

The book of Acts gives us a history, not a definition, of the church practice. In Acts some elders are established, and in Acts 6 some persons are appointed, but just by Acts alone we do not know that they are deacons. In addition, we do not know what kind of persons the elders should be and in what way they should be established. Without 1 Timothy through Philemon we are almost in darkness concerning the practice of the church. Philippians 1:1 mentions the overseers and deacons in the church, but there is no record of how they were produced or what kind of persons they were. Therefore, following the section concerning the matters of life, there are four books dealing with the practical side of the church life.

First Timothy 3:15 says, "But if I delay, I write that you may know how one ought to conduct himself in the house of God." This verse reveals the subject of these four books. Here the apostle Paul says that he may delay, but in principle the Lord is also delaying His coming. While the Lord is delaying His coming, these few books help us to know how to conduct ourselves in the church life. Although many matters are covered in the books through 2 Thessalonians, including the Lord's coming, the Lord did not intend to come immediately. If the Lord had intended to return right away, there would have been no need for these four books. While the Lord delays His coming and is keeping us on the earth to be the church, these four books tell us how to conduct ourselves in the house of God.

Even though these books give us instructions about the practice of the church life, many people do not pay adequate attention to them and thus miss the mark, making the secondary things to be primary, even making the last things to be first. The foremost matter that these four books speak of is how to conduct ourselves in the house of God. This is a matter of practice.

INSTRUCTIONS FOR PRACTICING THE CHURCH LIFE

The full and complete instructions for practicing the church life are in these four books. They tell us how to set up the government of the church, how to appoint and establish the elders, how to arrange the church service as the responsibility of the deacons, and how to learn many things by exercise and teach them to others (1 Tim. 3:1-13, 4:6-16; 2 Tim. 2:2). Whereas the first section, the nine books from Romans to 2 Thessalonians, is full of teaching, definition, and explanation, there is not much instruction. The four books of the second section, however, present many instructions but not much doctrinal teaching. This may be compared to a class: After a professor gives a lecture, he instructs the students how to practice in the laboratory.

Paul's Epistles to Timothy, Titus, and Philemon are full of instructions, not doctrines and definitions. In Romans there are not many instructions; mainly there are "lectures" with many definitions. It is the same with all the books through 2 Thessalonians. No doubt there are some instructions, but these books present mainly the definition and meaning of the church as the Body of Christ. The following four books give us the instructions on how to practice according to the definitions. Moreover, all the instructions in these books are very personal. Instructions given by an intimate tutor to his dear learners must be personal.

As to the church, we must first learn to know its life aspect. We must spend more time in the first nine books to experience what is taught and what is defined on the life side. Then, we must take care of another important matter, the practice of the church life according to the teachings of life. If we keep this in mind, the meaning of these four books will shine out when we read them.

EXERCISING UNTO GODLINESS

A key verse in these books is 1 Timothy 3:15, which gives us the main subject of this second section. First Timothy 4:7-8 are also key verses, speaking of our spiritual exercise. Verse 7 says, "Exercise yourself unto godliness." Godliness includes all spiritual matters, all the things relating to God and to our relationship with God. All these spiritual matters require exercise. We have to exercise in prayer, exercise in the study of the Word, exercise to visit people, and exercise in how to talk with people. We also must exercise to know how to use the words of the Scriptures as weapons to fight the battle, how to conduct ourselves in the meetings, how to fast for the sake of prayer, how to know the inner life, how to discern the spirit from the soul, and how to know the hymns. Godliness includes many items; it includes everything relating to God and especially relating to our relationship with God. Although *exercise unto godliness* is a short phrase, it is very profound.

We should ask ourselves how much we exercise. In today's Christian churches there is very little exercise. Some set up a seminary or Bible college for a small number of people to study the spiritual things, but with the church in general there may be no exercise. As a rule, what we see in many so-called churches is mainly the preaching of message after message without exercise. In the proper church life there must be the teaching and the exercise. This is the reason that after many years we have found the secret: We very much stress training. The church needs training. The way we take for the ministry in the church must include the way of the four books from 1 Timothy to Philemon, the way of exercise.

A brother who studied for his Ph.D. in chemistry told us that one lecture in class required ten times more work in the laboratory. His professor would say, "What is the good of a lecture? Listening makes you proud, but practice makes you humble." This is a good proverb. If we sit and listen to someone speak year after year, we may think that we know everything, and we can easily criticize everyone. Because of this, no one would dare to minister to us. If someone comes to minister, we may just listen and criticize his word, his teaching, and his attitude. It is easy to know things, but it is difficult to put them into practice.

Instead of criticizing someone, we should try to do a better job than he does; then we will be clear, and we will be humbled. I have learned this secret. Whenever a brother or sister criticizes something, I do not argue. I simply say, "Very good, brother. You take the responsibility to do it." If someone says the chairs are arranged wrongly or the piano is played poorly, we may say, "You are completely right. You come to do it." When we try to practice something, we realize how hard it is.

It is not easy to do things practically. The way to subdue those who criticize is to let them try to do the job themselves. In the early 1950s, I gave the saints many teachings along the line of life. The same brother who studied chemistry suggested that we should put all these matters into practice, and that if we did not, the saints would have all these points in their mind but not in reality. I agreed with him and told him to carry this out. He spent much time to write instructions and to put all these lessons into practical form. Then he trained the leading ones of the small groups how to practice and how to bring the saints in their groups into the same practice. This truly worked, and it helped us very much. This is the right principle. We need to exercise unto godliness.

TEACHING THOSE WHO WILL BE COMPETENT TO TEACH OTHERS

Second Timothy 2:2 says, "And the things which you have heard from me through many witnesses, these commit to faithful men, who will be competent to teach others also." Timothy learned many things from Paul and exercised them accordingly. Now he was charged by Paul to commit all that he had learned to others, who in turn would be competent to teach others. This is the training of the teachers, as in a teachers' college, which requires exercise, practice, and learning. As a church grows and the number increases, there is the need of practical instruction. This practical instruction cannot be put into practice in a large congregation. To a large congregation we can only give lectures and messages. In order to put all these things into practice, there is the need of smaller groups of ten or twenty to come together with one or two leading ones who know how to train the saints and bring them into the practice.

According to the instruction of the apostle Paul, Timothy cared for the work of training teachers, faithful men who were competent to teach others also. Timothy first learned from the apostle Paul, and then what he heard, he practiced. Following this, he passed it on to others. When we teach others, we learn more. Much of what I have learned came from teaching others. The principle is that wherever we minister, we should produce disciples. We should not minister all the time and yet not raise up others who can minister. After we minister for a while in a certain place, some who are competent to teach others should be produced by our ministry. The main thought of this section of the Epistles is that we need instruction in order to know how to conduct ourselves in the church. To do so, there is the need of an appointment or arrangement for the elders, deacons, and deaconesses. There is also the need to exercise unto godliness. All spiritual matters require a certain amount of exercise; even in choosing a hymn, we need to exercise. Then we also need to learn. We should not say that because we have the Holy Spirit within us, we can do everything. We also need to teach others, and if possible, we should try to have a small "teachers' college" to train others to be teachers, because in the practice of the church there is the need to produce more useful persons. These matters—appointment, arrangement, exercise, learning, and teaching others to be teachers—are the main matters of instruction found in the four books from 1 Timothy to Philemon.

Here we cannot go into much detail concerning these matters, but we can receive the principles. The New Testament always gives us the principles, but it leaves us the room to seek the present guidance of the Lord according to the situation. There is no need to copy anything outwardly. While we have the principle, we need to pray and consider according to the situation, the present need, and the Lord's leading. Even when we study something in class, we still need the practical application in the laboratory; then we will learn to carry it out in a better way.

PRACTICING THE CHURCH LIFE BY THE INNER LIFE

Although these four books give us instructions for the practice of the church life, they still stress the inner life. There are a number of important points about the inner life in these books, because in his instructions Paul often refers to life. The matters that we put into practice must be practiced in life. We dare not set up a seminary because that is merely a place to practice things for the sake of practice. Instead of a seminary we need a home. A seminary is based on knowledge, while the basic matter in a home is the life of the family. The practice of the church life must be based on life; it cannot be practiced without life. Although these books do not give us definitions concerning life, they give us many points relating to the inner life.

Having a Good Conscience and a Pure Heart

In these books, the apostle very much stresses a good conscience. According to the context of 1 Timothy 1:5, the practice of the church is a matter not of mere teachings but of love, which issues from a good conscience. In verse 19 Paul says, "Holding faith and a good conscience, concerning which some, thrusting these away, have become shipwrecked regarding the faith." Second Timothy 1:3 says, "I thank God, whom I serve from my forefathers in a pure conscience." This is not only a good conscience but a pure conscience. When we practice the church life, we need both a good conscience and a pure conscience. Furthermore, 1 Timothy 4:2 says, "By means of the hypocrisy of men who speak lies, of men who are branded in their own conscience as with a hot iron." These persons make their conscience to have no feeling; the sense, the consciousness, of their conscience has been destroyed. By reading all these verses, we can realize how much we need a good, pure, and sensitive conscience for the practice of the church life. First Timothy 1:5 also tells us that we need "love out of a pure heart." The heart as well as the conscience must be pure.

Being Empowered by Christ

First Timothy 1:12 says, "I give thanks to Him who empowers me, Christ Jesus our Lord." The word *empower* in Greek comes from the root word for *dynamo*. It is the same root word used in Philippians 4:13, which says, "I am able to do all things in Him who empowers me." Christ is the One who empowers us. In the practice of the church life, we must learn to be empowered by Christ. We should not merely do things outwardly according to certain regulations or forms.

We must do things from within by being empowered by Christ.

The Church as the House of the Living God, the Pillar and Base of the Truth, and the Mystery of Godliness

First Timothy 3:15-16 are great verses in the holy Scriptures. Verse 15 says, "But if I delay, I write that you may know how one ought to conduct himself in the house of God, which is the church of the living God, the pillar and base of the truth." Everything in the church must be living because this is the house of the living God. We should not do anything in the church according to dead rules or dead forms. Everything we do or practice in the church life must be living because we are serving a living God.

The church is also the pillar and base of the truth. This refers to the Triune God. The truth, the reality, is Christ, and Christ is the embodiment of God. As the pillar and base, therefore, the church bears the reality of the Triune God. The church stands not for doctrine but for the truth, the reality of the Triune God.

Verse 16 continues, "And confessedly, great is the mystery of godliness: He who was manifested in the flesh, / Justified in the Spirit, / Seen by angels, / Preached among the nations, / Believed on in the world, / Taken up in glory." God manifested in the flesh is the greatest mystery, the mystery of godliness.

The foregoing items are the main points related to the inner life. In order to practice the church life, we need to learn these instructions. Although we need the teachings, we must practice and learn them in the living God and in the fact that the church is the testimony of Jesus, the pillar and base of the truth, and the mystery of godliness, which is God manifested in the flesh.

In the Eternal Life and by the Heavenly Kingdom

First Timothy 6:12 says, "Lay hold on the eternal life." Whatever we intend to do, we must do in the eternal life.

In 2 Timothy 4:18 Paul says, "The Lord will deliver me from every evil work and will save me into His heavenly kingdom." In the same chapter he says, "I solemnly charge you before God and Christ Jesus, who is to judge the living and the dead, and by His appearing and His kingdom" (v. 1). The apostle Paul learned to experience Christ as his life, empowering him all the time, and he learned to practice the mystery of godliness. He also put the heavenly kingdom always before him as a goal. He was pressing on toward the goal for the kingdom, and at the end of his race he said that the Lord would save him into His heavenly kingdom. Therefore, he charged Timothy by His kingdom. We must be empowered within by Christ as our power, and we must also be warned and attracted by His heavenly kingdom.

If we read the New Testament carefully, we will see that the heavenly kingdom in its manifestation is a reward to the faithful overcomers who run the race and finish in victory. Second Timothy 4:7-8 says, "I have fought the good fight; I have finished the course; I have kept the faith. Henceforth there is laid up for me the crown of righteousness, with which the Lord, the righteous Judge, will recompense me in that day, and not only me but also all those who have loved His appearing." This is also an aspect of the inner life. We must realize that one day the Lord will appear to reward His servants, so we must fight, run, and keep the faith.

By the Superabounding Grace

First Timothy 1:14 says, "And the grace of our Lord superabounded with faith and love in Christ Jesus." The grace of the Lord was with Paul, all the time imparting faith and love into him. Strictly speaking, this grace is the Lord Himself. The practice of the church life must be in grace, in the inner empowering, in the living God, in the reality which the church stands for, in the mystery of godliness, in the eternal life, with a pure conscience and a pure heart, and in the life of the heavenly kingdom.

By the Lord with Our Spirit

Finally, 2 Timothy 4:22 says, "The Lord be with your spirit. Grace be with you." This word concludes these two books of instruction on the practice of the church. When we close a letter, we often use particular words with a definite meaning. Of all Paul's Epistles, there is only one that closes in this exact way. He did this with a definite purpose. No matter what kind of practice we may have or what kind of teaching we give, it must be something of the living Christ within our spirit. Although the practice, learning, and teaching of the church life is outward, there also must be something issuing from the indwelling Christ in our spirit. We should not merely have the outward practice and outward teaching. We must learn to practice all the things of the church life from a strengthened spirit.

CHAPTER TWENTY-THREE

THE PRACTICE OF THE CHURCH LIFE IN TITUS AND PHILEMON

Scripture Reading: Titus 2:14; Philem. 1-25

THE PRACTICE OF THE CHURCH LIFE IN TITUS

A Confirmation of 1 and 2 Timothy

Following the two books to Timothy, there is still the need of the short Epistle to Titus. Apparently this book is nearly the same as 1 and 2 Timothy, although it is not as complete, but it is still part of the holy Scriptures. What then is the purpose of Paul's letter to Titus? It is a principle that with all important matters and main points in the Scriptures, there is the need of confirmation. The book of Titus is a repetition of Paul's Epistles to Timothy to serve as confirmation that at least two young co-workers of the apostle Paul received the same kind of instruction.

The principle in the Scriptures is that a testimony must be borne by at least two or three witnesses. Therefore, after the two books of Timothy, there is the book to Titus. Not only do these books confirm each other, but the two recipients, Timothy and Titus, also could confirm each other. After the apostle Paul passed away, these two young co-workers were still alive. If only one of them had received instruction from Paul, there would not be a testimony or confirmation for that instruction. However, since there were two persons who received the same instruction, if someone rose up to argue and dispute an issue, Timothy and Titus could be a strong confirmation for one another and for the instructions themselves.

A Particular Christian Walk and Church Practice

Nevertheless, there is at least one matter found in Titus which is not mentioned in the Epistles to Timothy. Verse 14 of chapter two says, "Who gave Himself for us that He might redeem us from all lawlessness and purify to Himself a particular people as His unique possession, zealous of good works." *A particular people* is a special term in the New Testament. We should be particular not only in the inner life but also in our church practice. We should not follow the system of the world, and we should not make the practice of the church life a common thing that fits our human concept. Both our Christian walk and our practice of the church must be particular.

To be particular is to be different from the common way. Because we are a particular people living on the earth, our walk, our worship, and our service to God must not be common, according to the common system or on the common course. Of course, there is no need to be purposely peculiar, but if we go on not according to the traditional teachings but according to the Lord's inner, living guidance, we will automatically be different from the common worldly system. No matter how good the worldly system is, it is still according to the course of this age, and as such it is no doubt of Satan. Our walk and our church practice, however, must be out from God. God must be the source, the nature, and the origin of our particular walk, life, and practice. Whatever we have must be something of God and one hundred percent different from the worldly system and contradictory to the course of this age. The worldly system, the course of the age, are of the devil, but we are following the inner guidance of the Lord; therefore, we are spontaneously different.

We must try our best not to be influenced by the Christianity which we have seen. For nearly two thousand years, Christianity has been drifting away from God's particular divine nature. Therefore, we should not trust in the things of Christianity. We should put a big question mark on them. We must lay these things aside and come back to the Lord and to His Word, to study His Word and seek His guidance in all things. If possible, we should practice the church life outside of so-called Christianity. The only things in which we should be the same as Christianity are those things that are entirely from the Spirit and from the Lord's Word. We must go along, not with tradition, but with the inner guidance and the teaching of the Scriptures.

BROTHERLY LOVE
FOR THE CHURCH LIFE IN PHILEMON

By the Lord's sovereignty, the short book of Philemon comes at the end of the section on the practice of the church life. The significance of this book is that for the practice of the church life we need to keep brotherly love. Although other portions of the Scriptures teach us about brotherly love and loving one another, Philemon serves as an illustration, an example, of brotherly love. In the practice of the church life, the proper brotherly love is a real test. If we do not have the genuine brotherly love, we are spiritually dead. The proper, real, and true brotherly love is the test of whether we are living or dead. This is a love which surpasses ordinary human love in society.

In this book there are two persons. One is the master, Philemon, who has the full right of ownership of his slave, Onesimus. Unlike today in America, at Paul's time there was a custom that people could buy a person as a slave. The master who purchased a slave had the right to do anything with him, including to put the slave to death. That was not illegal; the law gave him the right to do so. Onesimus was a slave who was owned by Philemon, a wealthy brother. However, Onesimus had run away from his master, and according to the custom in those times an escaped slave could be put to death. For this reason, Onesimus was put into prison, but while he was in prison, he met Paul, the messenger of the Lord. This means that he met the Lord, because in this book Paul represents the Lord Himself. As a result, Onesimus was saved (v. 10). Following this, Paul sent him back to his master, Philemon, and entreated Philemon to treat Onesimus as a beloved brother (vv. 12-16). From this time forward Philemon would have Onesimus no longer as a slave but as a brother.

This is an illustration of brotherly love which surpasses all the practices in human society. Hence, in the church life we must have such a brotherly love. The principle in Philemon is that in the practice of the church there must be a brotherly love that overcomes all the differences in human society. If brotherly love can overcome the difference in social rank between a slave and a master, then it is able to overcome all the differences in human society. The differences and ranks in human society must not be brought into the practice of the church life. In the church practice all the differences in society are excluded.

It is difficult for brothers or sisters who have a high position in human society to practice brotherly love. If a brother is a president or a king, it may be difficult for him to properly practice being a brother in the church. Therefore, it is better not to be a president or a king. According to the history of the church throughout the centuries, bringing social rank into the practice of the church has been a great problem. When differences of rank in human society are brought into the practice of the church, the nature of the church is changed. This damages and spoils the proper practice of the church life. This is the very reason that the book of Philemon is found at the end of this section of the New Testament. In the proper practice of the church we can never neglect brotherly love.

We must shut the door of the church to all social rank in human society. There is no place in the church for the "uniforms" of social rank. We should not come to the church with the "uniform" of an admiral, a marshal, or a medical doctor. To bring these things into the church will damage the church life. How much we have the reality of the church life is tested by our brotherly love. This is not a small or easy matter. If someone attains to a high office, he will see the difficulty it causes; it will be hard for him to come down from his "throne."

Even in the United States, the problem of social rank is serious. Formerly I thought that in America all people had the same status. Recently, however, an officer in the armed forces told me that it is not easy for him to contact enlisted men, because they do not have the same rank. It is also difficult for the wife of an officer to come down off her "throne" to talk with the wife of an enlisted man. This also is due to the difference in rank. One Christian brother told me that while he was serving in the air force, he had the burden to open his home to fellow soldiers who were brothers, but his wife would not agree. She said that to do this would lower his status. Wives such as this want to maintain their social rank. In this respect, the United States may be better than other countries, but even in this country there is the problem of social rank.

We must overcome this problem by the inner life. We need to receive the Lord's demand to receive Onesimus. Even a slave can become a dear brother to us. However, if we feel we are different from such a brother, if it is hard to humble ourselves to sit with him, we must be reminded that we are wrong. We should sit alongside such a brother just as we would sit with the apostle Paul. We need to realize that regardless of his rank, he is our dear brother. In the practice of the church life, we need to learn this basic principle, which will correct, adjust, and balance us. Therefore, Philemon is not a book of teaching; it is a book of instruction, instructing us how to treat our brothers who are of lower social rank in human society.

A SUMMARY OF THE REMAINING BOOKS
OF THE NEW TESTAMENT

The Eight Supplementary Books

As we have seen, the thirteen books from Romans to Philemon are the definition of the Body of Christ. In this definition, there is the aspect of teaching and the aspect of instruction, the side of life and the side of practice. It seems that these books are complete. Why then is there the need to have another group of eight Epistles: Hebrews, James, 1 and 2 Peter, John's three Epistles, and Jude? The first group of thirteen Epistles were all written by one apostle, Paul, giving us a full definition of the Body of the universal man, the church, on the two sides of life and practice. The latter group, however, was written by a composition of writers, including Paul, James, Peter, John, and Jude. These books are not, strictly speaking, directly related to the definition of the church. Rather, they are supplementary in nature.

Christ and Judaism in Hebrews

The first book of this group is Hebrews, which shows us the difference between Christ and Judaism. There is the need of this book to help Christians, especially the Jewish Christians, know the position of the Old Testament and Judaism. This supplementary book makes it very clear that the things in the Old Testament and Judaism are types and shadows. The body, the reality, is Christ Himself. When the reality comes, there is no need to hold on to the shadows, the types; we should put them away. The Old Testament is simply a type of Christ, and since Christ, the reality, has come, the type must be put away. This is the purpose of the book of Hebrews.

Faith and Works in James

The book of James is also a supplement, showing us the relationship between faith and works. It adjusts the wrong concept concerning faith, telling us that the proper, living faith must be followed and proved by works and it should produce works. This balance and adjustment in our understanding of faith is very important in the Christian life.

The Government of God in 1 and 2 Peter

Without the proper help, we may read 1 and 2 Peter for a long time without knowing what they are about. The subject of these books is important yet mysterious and hard to perceive. The concepts of suffering, the cross, and judgment are found in these two books, but this is not the central thought. Rather, these two books reveal the mysterious, divine government of God. Many of the sufferings we experience are due to God's government, and judgment is also related to God's government. Because God governs, He judges. In the first thirteen Epistles, Paul does not deal with this point very much, so there is the need for 1 and 2 Peter as a supplement. We can see the government of God in every chapter of these books.

Many of our circumstances come from God's government. According to God's government, we must abide by certain rules. If we do not keep these rules, we will suffer. We can compare this to the government in the United States. If we do not obey the laws and regulations of the federal and state governments, we will have trouble. When we drive a car, we have to drive according to the traffic regulations. To get a traffic ticket after neglecting a stop sign is a matter of government. In the same way, as the children of God we need to keep the rules and the regulations of the divine government.

Many sufferings come because of the divine government. Many times we suffer because we are wrong; we are violating the regulations and laws of God's government. In the universe today there is such a thing as the government of God. Whether or not people respect it, the government of God is still here. We all must learn this. The entire contents of these two books prove to us that even today, before the manifestation of the kingdom, during this age of rebellion on the earth among mankind, and even among Christians, God still has His government.

The most significant verse in 1 Peter is found in 4:17, which says, "For it is time for the judgment to begin from the house of God; and if first from us, what will be the end of those who disobey the gospel of God?" This refers to the government of God. The supplement of 1 and 2 Peter tells us that we, the people of God, must realize that there is a divine government in the universe. We should not be ignorant or foolish; we must respect God's government today.

The Divine Fellowship in the Epistles of John

The three Epistles of John are a supplement concerning the fellowship in the divine family, a point which was not thoroughly covered in the definition of the Body of Christ given in the first thirteen Epistles. John's three Epistles show us how God's children fellowship with the Father and with one another in the Father's family. The word *fellowship* is the most important word in these three books. In 1 John 1 the eternal life is preached and ministered to us (vv. 1-3). When we receive the eternal life, the issue is fellowship with one another and with the Father and His Son.

Dealing with Apostasy in Jude

The short book of Jude is a supplement to deal with apostasy, which was not dealt with in the first thirteen Epistles.

Five matters—Judaism, works and faith, the government of God, the divine fellowship, and apostasy—are all dealt with in these last eight Epistles. In total, there are twenty-one Epistles. Thirteen of these define the Body of the universal man, and the remaining eight are a supplement to make us clear about the above five matters. Without these eight books, we still have a full definition of the church, the nature of the church, the fellowship of the church, the responsibility of the church, and the practice of the church life. However, we are not clear about the position of Judaism and the Old Testament. Neither do we know the relationship between faith and works, God's government in the universe, the divine fellowship in God's family, and apostasy. Because this supplement of eight books is added to the Epistles, every matter is covered, and there are no unanswered questions.

Revelation as the Consummation of the Entire Scriptures

Following these eight books, there is Revelation as the ultimate consummation and conclusion of the New Testament and the entire Scriptures. This long book of twenty-two chapters speaks clearly about three main points. The first main point is found in the first three chapters, which present the vision of the local churches existing on the earth to be the golden lampstands as the testimony of Jesus. This is the accomplishment of God's eternal intention and purpose.

The third main point is found in the last two chapters, chapters twenty-one and twenty-two. Here we have a picture of the work of God for the fulfillment of His eternal purpose, which consummates in a building. In nature, in principle, and in nearly every aspect, this building is exactly the same as the golden lampstands in chapters one through three. The local churches are the local lampstands, and this building is a universal lampstand. The entire city of New Jerusalem is a great golden lampstand; Christ, the Lamb, is the lamp on this stand; and God in Christ is the light (21:23). This is the great, universal, unique, and ultimate lampstand. Whereas all the local churches are the golden lampstands in time, the great, universal, unique lampstand is in eternity. In eternity there will be one unique lampstand in the entire universe, but in time on this earth today in each locality of human society, there is a golden lampstand. The local lampstands are the same in nature, in life, in function, and in almost every aspect as the unique, great, universal lampstand.

At the two ends of Revelation there are the first and third main points. Then from chapters four to twenty there is a long section containing God's judgment. This is the second main point. God judges all things which do not correspond with the unique lampstand. After the Lord accomplished redemption, He ascended to the heavens; it is at this time that God's judgment began. Revelation 4 through 20 is a long record starting from the time of the Lord's ascension until the time of His second coming. This period of time is a dispensation of not only the gospel but of judgment. On the one hand, throughout the past two thousand years God has been propagating the gospel to the fallen race, but on the other hand, He has constantly been judging.

One of the first items of God's judgment was the destruction of Jerusalem in A.D. 70. God sent the army of Titus, the prince of the Roman Empire, to destroy that Jewish city, because the system of Judaism, although it was religious and good, did not correspond with the lampstands. With this viewpoint, we can understand the history both of the church and of the world. Century after century, God has judged those things that do not correspond to His church. The Roman Empire, the Spanish Empire, and even the British Empire were judged by God because they did not correspond with the lampstand. Therefore, we should be warned and reminded that everything we have must correspond to the testimony of the church.

Today God is using even the communist governments to judge certain things, but I have the full assurance that one day God will turn around and judge communism. This is similar to what He did in the Old Testament. God used Assyria and Babylon to judge other nations, including Israel, but afterward He turned around and judged these empires.

According to the book of Revelation, God is seeking after only one thing—the Body of Christ, the church, the lampstand as the testimony of Jesus. Anything that does not correspond to this, God will judge and burn with fire. Eventually, everything that does not correspond to the church will be burned in the lake of fire. On the contrary, all things which correspond to the testimony of the church will be in the New Jerusalem. There are only two issues for all things: the lake of fire and the New Jerusalem.

A WORD OF FELLOWSHIP CONCERNING TRAINING

What we have seen thus far of a general sketch of the New Testament should be considered as a training. You must now spend several years to try to put what you have seen into practice.

Not Making Demands on Others

In addition, you must never put demands on any person, church, or group according to what you have received. To put demands on others or on the church is not a help; rather, it is a great damage. If you want to make demands, make demands on yourself. Do not say to others, "Now my eyes are opened. We have been trained in a certain way, but you don't have this. Therefore, the church here is too poor." Demanding never helps the situation. The right thing to do is to supply and minister.

The training meetings are completely different from the church meetings. It is a problem when some do not differentiate the two kinds of meetings. The one who conducts a training has the ground to say certain things to the trainees, but you do not have the same ground with others. If you speak things in the same way as in a training meeting, you may damage the situation. Therefore, do not treat other people as trainees. You may treat only yourself as a trainee. This is a serious matter. On the mainland of China, some brothers after being trained became a great help to the local churches, but others went back to their localities and became a big damage. They treated the church as their trainees, and they made demands on the church. This is wrong. You are not trained to make people your trainees. Rather, you are trained to grow, to minister, and to supply something from the Lord. You are trained even to suffer loss for others.

Not Criticizing or Causing Divisions

In addition, whenever you make a demand, you are tempted to criticize. You may realize the true situation with others, but do not criticize them. Do not believe in yourself too much when you see the situation, because your realization about it may not be correct. Apparently a person's situation is of one kind, but in actuality it may be of another kind, so it is foolish to discern things too fast. Be careful in speaking about a situation. Just consider how easy it is for others to misunderstand you. In the same way, you may feel that a certain brother is not right, but before the Lord he may be very right. Therefore, we must be careful.

After we are trained, our eyes are opened to a certain extent, and it is easy for us to discern things according to our new understanding. As a result, we are tempted first to criticize others and then to cause divisions. This is one hundred percent wrong. Never go to a place or remain in your place to discern things according to your training and then criticize and make divisions. If you do this, you will never be a help to the church. Rather, you will damage it.

Supplying the Body

Learn to be humble, faithful, and honest, and always do your best not to contradict. Always do your best to minister help to others in a quiet way without contradicting. In this way you will supply nourishment, solid food, to the Body. The Body needs this. There is no need to adjust others. If there is something wrong in the Body, the supply will take care of it spontaneously. The supply is like a dose of medicine. If you administer the dose, the medicine will eventually get into the Body. Then if there is a germ, some element in the medicine will kill it unconsciously.

In the past I have said that you must be aggressive, and that is right. However, I now advise you to not be a trouble-maker in the church. This is very important. As those who have been trained, we must be careful.

Not Forcing Others, but Ministering Christ

Lastly, you may stress certain matters, but do not force them on others. When people are ready to receive something, take the opportunity to minister something, but if they are not ready, you should not go too fast. Simply pray and wait. You must be strong, but do not be forceful. Go along with the situation and wait for the Lord. If what you do is of the Lord, He will prepare the way. When He prepares the proper situation, that is the time to minister something.

Caring for the Unique Expression of the Church in a Locality

Remember that the expression of the church in a locality must be unique. Therefore, we all need to keep the oneness, and in order to keep the oneness you must learn not to damage or make trouble. Rather, always minister something positive of life, something of Christ, and let it work in people to deal with the negative things.

I beg you to keep these few matters in mind. This will help you and help the local churches wherever you are and wherever you go. Always learn to be a help to the church and never to create trouble. Because the local expression of the church is one, you have no other way to take. You cannot act independently or outside the local expression. Whether or not you are happy with a local church, you must go along with it. Learn to submit yourself to the present situation of the local church where you are. May the Lord be merciful to us. We all must learn to be wise and humble, and we must do our best to be a real help.

Three Needful Matters for the Church

In my heart I am truly burdened for the church in three matters. First, we must know the inner life, that is, know Christ in a living way. Second, we must have the proper church life so that Christ may be exalted and expressed. Third, we need to preach the gospel, to do our best to bring unbelievers to the Lord, to win their souls at any cost, spending ourselves and being willing to sacrifice everything that we have. We must endeavor by the mercy and grace of the Lord to care equally for these three things. This is the right way. There is no need to care for mere doctrines, teachings, or other matters. We should care mainly for the above three matters.

ABOUT THE AUTHOR

Witness Lee was born in 1905 in northern China and raised in a Christian family. At age 19 he was fully captured for Christ and immediately consecrated himself to preach the gospel for the rest of his life. Early in his service, he met Watchman Nee, a renowned preacher, teacher, and writer. Witness Lee labored together with Watchman Nee under his direction. In 1934 Watchman Nee entrusted Witness Lee with the responsibility for his publication operation, called the Shanghai Gospel Bookroom.

Prior to the Communist takeover in 1949, Witness Lee was sent by Watchman Nee and his other co-workers to Taiwan to ensure that the things delivered to them by the Lord would not be lost. Watchman Nee instructed Witness Lee to continue the former's publishing operation abroad as the Taiwan Gospel Bookroom, which has been publicly recognized as the publisher of Watchman Nee's works outside China. Witness Lee's work in Taiwan manifested the Lord's abundant blessing. From a mere 350 believers, newly fled from the mainland, the churches in Taiwan grew to 20,000 in five years.

In 1962 Witness Lee felt led of the Lord to come to the United States, settling in California. During his 35 years of service in the U.S., he ministered in weekly meetings and weekend conferences, delivering several thousand spoken messages. Much of his speaking has since been published as over 400 titles. Many of these have been translated into over fourteen languages. He gave his last public conference in February 1997 at the age of 91.

He leaves behind a prolific presentation of the truth in the Bible. His major work, *Life-study of the Bible,* comprises over 25,000 pages of commentary on every book of the Bible from the perspective of the believers' enjoyment and experience of God's divine life in Christ through the Holy Spirit. Witness Lee was the chief editor of a new translation of the New Testament into Chinese called the Recovery Version and directed the translation of the same into English. The Recovery Version also appears in a number of other languages. He provided an extensive body of footnotes, outlines, and spiritual cross references. A radio broadcast of his messages can be heard on Christian radio stations in the United States. In 1965 Witness Lee founded Living Stream Ministry, a non-profit corporation, located in Anaheim, California, which officially presents his and Watchman Nee's ministry.

Witness Lee's ministry emphasizes the experience of Christ as life and the practical oneness of the believers as the Body of Christ. Stressing the importance of attending to both these matters, he led the churches under his care to grow in Christian life and function. He was unbending in his conviction that God's goal is not narrow sectarianism but the Body of Christ. In time, believers began to meet simply as the church in their localities in response to this conviction. In recent years a number of new churches have been raised up in Russia and in many eastern European countries.